A New Deal for Teachers

A New Deal for Teachers

Accountability the Public Wants, Authority the Teachers Need

Curtis Johnson

ROWMAN & LITTLEFIELD
Lanham • Boulder • New York • London

Published by Rowman & Littlefield
An imprint of The Rowman & Littlefield Publishing Group, Inc.
4501 Forbes Boulevard, Suite 200, Lanham, Maryland 20706
www.rowman.com

6 Tinworth Street, London, SE11 5AL, United Kingdom

Copyright © 2021 by Curtis Johnson

All rights reserved. No part of this book may be reproduced in any form or by any electronic or mechanical means, including information storage and retrieval systems, without written permission from the publisher, except by a reviewer who may quote passages in a review.

British Library Cataloguing in Publication Information Available

Library of Congress Cataloging-in-Publication Data

Names: Johnson, Curtis, 1942– author.
Title: A new deal for teachers : accountability the public wants, authority the teachers need / Curtis Johnson.
Description: Lanham, Maryland : Rowman & Littlefield, 2021. | Includes bibliographical references and index. | Summary: "This book outlines a steadily growing teacher-powered movement, now in 20 states of the U.S., that finds teachers in charge of what matters for student and school success"—Provided by publisher.
Identifiers: LCCN 2020045793 (print) | LCCN 2020045794 (ebook) | ISBN 9781475853100 (cloth) | ISBN 9781475853117 (paperback) | ISBN 9781475853124 (ebook)
Subjects: LCSH: Educational accountability—United States. | Teaching, Freedom of—United States.
Classification: LCC LB2806.22 .J65 2021 (print) | LCC LB2806.22 (ebook) | DDC 371.14/40973—dc23
LC record available at https://lccn.loc.gov/2020045793
LC ebook record available at https://lccn.loc.gov/2020045794

In memory of Neal Peirce

With whom I did three books and scores of feature newspaper articles over a quarter century. Neal Peirce, who wrote about cities and states for the Washington Post *Writers Group for nearly forty years, took my bloated, passive-voice-riddled graduate-school style and taught me to replace it with succinct leads, short paragraphs, and the occasional single-line zinger. He was not just a colleague. He was a teacher.*

Contents

Foreword ix
Preface xiii
Acknowledgments xvii
Introduction xxi

1 Imagine a Different School: Teaching as a Real Profession   1
2 Teachers Can Do It: Autonomy Is the Key   9
3 Trust the Teachers—Finally: The Movement Itself   25
4 Hit the Accelerator: How the Movement Could Grow   41
5 Rocks in the Road: Getting Past Obstacles   53
6 First Bird Off the Wire: Bargaining for What Future?   61
7 Conclusion   69

Epilogue   77
Bibliography   83
Index   89

Foreword

The idea of teachers running schools seems preposterous. Proper organizations have a leader, and a hierarchy of leaders creates efficient organizations whose operating procedures can be replicated, creating excellence for all. Or so we are told.

That worldview is in public education's DNA. School districts in the United States were largely born into the era of industrial production, and textbooks on school organization borrowed practices from that era's efficiency experts. The Los Angeles school district is a case in point, one whose history we follow in *Learning from L.A.* It was an icon of the Progressive Era school reforms of the early 20th century, and only in its final twenty years did the limitations of industrial design appear obvious.

Schools were never factories: Despite their bell schedules and thick policy documents, there was more than a little truth to the teacher refrain that "I'm in charge when the classroom door is closed." Nowhere is that more obvious than in this 2020 spring of pandemic operations. Teacher supervision, as it is generally understood, has been virtually nonexistent as faculty largely self-manage their transition to online classes.

Much of the academic literature in the field of organizational behavior addresses the failure of bureaucracies to perform as we think they should, and there has long been a fascination with network forms of organization and workers' cooperatives, both in the United States and other countries.

At the same time, the school district demonstrates the huge paradox of large organizations. It needs flexibility and nimbleness for teachers to do their work. At the same time, the capacity of the huge organization is playing a pivotal role in feeding Los Angeles during the stay-at-home orders. Its massive kitchens have expanded operations to cook not just for students but for their families and community members who would otherwise be food insecure.

So, bureaucracy persists even in the face of environmental pressures to operate differently. Assumptions that the postindustrial, knowledge work era would foster a new work environment proved overly optimistic. Large-scale reform efforts foundered in districts across the country.

In the 1990s, teacher unions and school managers began to forge new operating arrangements with more decentralization and elements of self-management for teachers—not just teachers in isolation but teachers as a collective. I believed then, and continue to believe, that teacher unions are the most potent political force for changing how teachers work.

But these arrangements are fragile. By the time that our book *A Union of Professionals* was published in 1993, many of the union-management joint ventures it chronicled were in tatters.

The historic fragility of self-governing organizations and schools built around networks makes the teacher-run schools in this book all the more interesting. These schools depart from the norms not just because the teachers demonstrate talent. For decades, scholars have written case studies of excellent teachers. Most of them are iconoclasts. They break rules, teach differently than the norm, and motivate students by getting them to think and act beyond the standard curriculum. Instead of leading their colleagues, they are often punished by their organizations and work as social isolates in their schools. In the schools Curtis Johnson writes about, called "teacher-powered" schools, the faculty band together.

Teacher-powered schools are not so much about what they don't have—an administrative hierarchy—as they are about teachers learning how to divide up authority and accountability. Teachers in these schools are not just good in their classrooms; they are good at getting organizational fundamentals right. They learn to make decisions without treating faculty meetings as street theater. They are good at distributing a school's precious resources of time and budget. They are good at evaluating one another's work in ways that are fair but tough minded.

But mostly, they are good at engaging students. The secret of teacher-powered schools is not that teachers get power but that they are able to empower students to take charge of their own learning. School is different in these schools, more hands-on, more engaging.

Not every teacher is ready for this. Not every school or district or teacher union is ready. But our times are ready-or-not-times. Covid-19 did not ask whether schools were ready to teach online, whether teachers were ready to assume a greater role in how they teach and interact with students. It simply challenged old assumptions about what is school and how students learn. While some may think that the current situation is only a temporary aberration, like a flood or hurricane, disrupting school operations for a few weeks or months, the weight of history suggests that schooling is at a pivot point. The new normal will not be a return to the old normal.

That makes the story that Curtis Johnson tells worth our attention.

—Charles Taylor Kerchner, professor emeritus,
Claremont Graduate University

Preface

The publication of this book was slowed as a consequence of the pandemic, with which Americans, along with many other people of the world, are coping. In late May of 2020, the eruptions around social justice, triggered by the killing of George Floyd by a police officer on the streets of Minneapolis, triggered fires and fury and forced a long overdue conversation about the way people of color have suffered from injustices in many systems. The chapters that follow—other than the Epilogue, which has been added—reflect these challenges with limited editing. But it is worth noting that every message in this book is more urgent, the case for turning to teachers for the schools of the future is more compelling, and the need for serious improvement in student learning is more obvious than ever before.

I do realize that any comment about the pandemic situation or the eruptions around racial unrest in the United States is the roughest of the first drafts of history. Clearly while we are all in it, we have trouble seeing any of the eventual consequences, though some seem, in keeping with the theme of this book, just too obvious.

It is perhaps too obvious that personalizing learning, something teachers do once they are in charge, is the key to reducing if not eliminating learning gaps. Everyone acknowledges that, to achieve the society we all say we want, and the economy this nation will need, we need everyone to be prepared to participate. But today we do not prepare everyone. Getting reorganized around this aim must become the norm. It may be too obvious that schools controlled by teachers are more likely to be innovators, to seize what technology makes possible, to be organized around what motivates students to learn.

In many interviews of people around the country, mostly people in the education industry, I found stark disbelief that teachers could actually, even collegially, take responsibility for a school's learning program. Someone has to be in charge, most told me. A school has to have a strong principal. Teachers need someone to tell them what to do; that was what many people said. Teachers do not want to lead, they claimed. They just want to teach. Those were just some of the responses I got to a simple question about the prospect of teachers running schools.

Having been involved for decades in the organizational network known as Education Evolving (EE), I witnessed the early proliferation of schools where teachers formed professional partnerships to have the biggest say in the school's approach to learning. EE now leads this national network of teacher-powered schools. I saw what a difference this simple but profound change seemed to make in student behavior. And it was clear to me that many teachers have been in the on-deck circle for a long time, waiting on this kind of opportunity. Teachers struck me as anything but average, as so many claimed they were.

It is true that some teachers just want to be left alone. But I find myself wondering why? Why do they not want that opportunity? So they can squeeze some professional autonomy into just the classroom? For some, it is just a job. That is true in any field. But for many the environment they find when they graduate from colleges of education is not anything like what they thought it would be. As one teacher put it to me in New York City, describing his first teaching job in another state, "They treated me like I didn't know anything."

In the chapters that follow, I cite the University of Pennsylvania professor Richard Ingersoll's research and writing. He is a leading academic who has an interest in the amount of influence teachers actually have in schools. When he published *Who Controls Teachers' Work?* in 2003, his blunt answer was: not teachers. And there is more research from John Shindler, Rachel Jean Eels, John Hedy, Roger Goddard, and Sara Kemper, who dedicated her doctoral dissertation to the subject. And while their research was largely surveys and field observations, significant credit is due Kim Farris-Berg and Ed Dirkswager for their work in writing *Trusting Teachers.* Finally, I should refer to Charles Kerchner, who has combined an interest in teaching with his academic research with a career-long curiosity about what teachers unions might do (see the Foreword).

Ingersoll started wondering, soon after he discovered a small movement of teachers in charge of schools, whether teachers in these partnerships would have an effect on student motivation. When he started looking, he found scant literature in the academic world even exploring this key question. Now it is a growing field.

You will also find many references to Ted Kolderie. He lives not far away, in Saint Paul, Minnesota. But wherever he was, I would have found him to be the most insightful and creative analyst of the education industry I ever knew. It helps to have spent his career in journalism and public policy. He often suggests that it's easier to see organizational structures, rather like physical structures—from the outside. This is the kind of public intellectual one rarely comes across, much less have a long relationship with. Because he has never been an educator, some dismiss him. They should not.

I must also mention the influence of Clayton Christensen, who died in January of 2020. Clay had been a professor in the Harvard Business School (HBS) since the mid-1990s. His book *The Innovator's Dilemma* in 1997 was the all-time best-selling modern business book. I was honored to help him write the 2008 book *Disrupting Class*.

The arguments with him and coauthor Michael Horn in Clay's HBS office were memorable; even more memorable were the stories he would tell, all priceless gems he forged from seeing the main dynamics in just about every organizational situation, then reducing those principles to an unforgettable story.

But, back to this book. Study after study names teachers as the key ingredient for student and school success. Yet we have to remember that what happens in school is really all about what happens to students. It is one thing for the teachers to have professional fulfillment, to be happy working in a particular school. But if the students do not catch the learning bug, if they do not want to be there, all is lost. For them and for society.

I am past the age when most people retire. I was president of three colleges, and before that, a teacher. I do understand what it means to be in a classroom, to feel responsible for whether students learn. I have been chief of staff to a governor and head of a large governmental organization, so I am not naïve about how difficult change can be.

And I have been a coauthor of four previous books—about metropolitan regions and, most recently, about how technology is changing the way young people learn. But this book, about the teacher-powered schools movement, is the most significant statement I have ever tried to make.

Having been one, I have no brief against educators. Most are earnest and hard-working people. But they are good people in a bad system. And the system that America has for schooling is simply not designed to give every child a decent chance to learn, to become what they have the potential to be. It is not the people; it is the system. And that is what the teacher professionalism initiative is aimed at: changing the system to get learning back to its inherent basics, while using everything that today's technology and advanced insights make possible.

We can get to better results for students. But only by trusting teachers. Only by letting those who are willing, even eager, to be in charge, take full control of their schools. That may be the long-elusive path to restoring the student motivation that pays off.

Acknowledgments

Let me begin by admitting that ceding control over schools to teachers was a heavy lift for a lot of people. It should not be so, but it is. I appreciate those who consented to talk to me and initially found the idea disruptive—maybe even destructive of the system they knew well—but acknowledged that the system does not work well for most young people, and that something ought to be done. That flexibility of mindset will prove crucial if this idea gets real traction and begins to take hold in American education.

I suppose that all authors thank their spouses. But doing so here is nothing but pure authenticity. My wife, Carol, and my gratitude are both great. She has been patient and supportive throughout the process of interviewing and writing. Then, I must mention Ted Kolderie, who has lectured and listened, who has read and reacted, who by phone and email and even regular mail has been a consistent contributor to whatever wisdom this book may have.

In the academic world, I must point to Charles Kerchner, the one academic I know who has occupied the intersection of education and unionism; he supplied the Foreword for this book. The other academic whose work has been indispensable is Richard Ingersoll, at the University of Pennsylvania. Richard has tolerated my many calls, provided studies that proved relevant, and been an outstanding colleague in thinking through what might unlock this movement to become even more consequential.

And right along with Richard was Amy Junge, who directs the teacher-powered movement for EE from her office in Southern California. Amy has provided names for interviews; she has thought through the growth process; and she read through multiple drafts of the manuscript, correcting mistakes and providing invaluable advice. Amy has been a teacher and remembers well the hope and special spirit that the best teachers have.

In the world of teacher unions, special thanks goes to John Wright, who brought both his perspective as a state leader and his more recent experience at the national level to bear on the central questions facing unions today at every level. And locally, former union heads Lynn Nordgren and Louise Sundin have given consistently good advice and have sought out vital connections for the cause.

Finding problems with an author's initial draft is always a tedious, often thankless, job. David Osborne, a friend and distinguished author, volunteered to read the manuscript, the publisher having pushed the pause button during the pandemic. Osborne's critique was especially helpful in making the case coherent and correcting potential misimpressions. I am grateful for his contributions.

I should also thank Ember Reichgott Junge, the former state senator who shepherded the nation's first chartering law through the legislative process and wrote the best book extant about the early years of the chartering movement. And Peter Hutchinson, who was always there for me to bounce once potentially crazy idea after another off his good head; his advice is always treasured.

And when Ananth Pai called me several years ago, I might have waved off someone less persistent. But his story and his vision of what school could be, if teachers were in charge, was compelling. His classroom—if that is what it is—was unforgettable. Michael Horn has been consulted extensively over the past decade. His advice and reactions were crucial to getting some controversial things right. And Sal Khan's webinars. Anyone who has experienced them knows why I appreciate what he says—and what he has done over the last decade and a half.

I began this project rather deeply convinced that schools where teachers were in charge of what matters were the best future we could imagine. At the end of the project, I am even more convinced this is true. Let us now see whether we can open this door for every group of willing teachers.

Finally, I want to thank everyone who agreed to be interviewed or with whom I had some conversation about this subject over recent years. A couple of them were observed and listened to in webinars. Most of them were in 2019. They are listed here in alphabetical order, but I am grateful to each one of them individually.

Bill Andrekopolous, Jeff Austin, Zaynab Baalbaki, Chris Barbic, Lincoln Bacal, Carrie Bakken, Parker Baxter, Jackie Bennett, Erik Berg, Jason Berg, Brad Blue, Candice Caroll Boben, Sally Ann Bongiovanni-Famularo, Drew Catt, Madeleine Ciolatti, Susanna Cordova, Walter Cortina, Frank Coyne, Kerry Decker, Edward Dirkswager, Josef Donnelly, Walter Enloe, Lars Esdal, Jake Fields, Shana Finnegan, Dan French, Howard Fuller, Dan Grego, Aaron Grimm, Jay Haugen, Rick Hess, Paul Hill, Erin Hinrichs, Bob Hoffman,

Michael Horn, Richard Ingersoll, Ember Reichgott-Junge, Brenda Martinez, Cris Parr, John Parr, Eric Premack, Jen Reedy, Amy Junge, Sara Kemper, Charles Kerchner, Lyle Kirtman, Alexander Kolokotronis, Emily Langhorne, Brent Maddin, Julie Mathiesen, John T. McCrann, Tim McDonald, Carol McFarlane, Dan Mott, Cindy Murphy, Joe Nathan, Lynn Nordgren, David Osborne, Ben Owens, Julene Oxton, Jeff Park, Dan Pickens, Mary Cathryn Ricker, Bill Ristow, Ted Sanders, Chris Sedati, Liz Seubert, Tony Simmons, Mary Sjoberg, Taryn Snyder, Daphne LaBleu Stenzel, Heather Stotts, Nathan Strenge, Louise Sundin, Dee Thomas, Doug Thomas, Thomas Toch, Paul Tweed, Adam Urbanski, Alex Vitrella, Robert Wedl, Nora Whalen, Scott Widmeyer, Arthur Wise, John Wright, and Lisa Wyatt.

Introduction

"Some things are too obvious." A longtime colleague, now departed, used to say that a lot. The notion that teachers should be in charge of a school and its learning strategy may well be one of those things.

Certainly, the idea of offering a "new deal" to teachers—one that offers authority that many teachers want for the accountability that the public demands—seems like it is designed for the teacher-powered movement.

Verne Johnson's comment about obvious things (said often when he was still vice president for strategy at General Mills) is a reminder of what happened when former Minnesota Governor Rudy Perpich asked Bill Andres, then the recently retired CEO of what was in the 1980s Dayton-Hudson Corporation (now Target), to chair a task force aimed at improving productivity in state government.

Andres responded with a question, "Is productivity something you do . . . or something that happens if you do the fundamentals right?" He went on to say that in retailing *turnover* was very important. Stores that turnover inventory are more profitable. But when a store manager tries to *do turnover*, the store is soon not profitable. So we decided at Dayton-Hudson, he went on, that turnover is something that happens if we do the fundamentals right.

So, applied to education, it follows that improvement is something that happens if you get the fundamentals right.

Teacher-powered schools, as they are now known, get the fundamentals right better than most schools in the enterprise of public education. In these schools teachers are in charge of what matters. They have the authority to make the decisions that matter most for students and schools.

But there is considerable disbelief that teachers could even want to be in charge of schools. Surveys (cited later) show otherwise. And note the reflections of Cris Parr, a career teacher in the Milwaukee Public Schools (top of chapter 1), who defied the odds people throw up—from districts to unions—and started new schools that were teacher-powered. This is how innovations spread: start small, let good things spread, and scale.

There are certainly good schools in the United States, all over. And good people working in schools. But the system itself was never designed to serve *all* the kids. And it does not. Today that stands out as never before. The system needs a redesign and the teacher-powered movement is ideally suited to be that new design.

Jack Frymier, long departed, lifelong educator and professor at Ohio State University, pointed to the pivotal importance of student engagement before it was fashionable to have these conversations. As he so often said, any successful effort to improve student learning will begin by improving student motivation. Motivation, he said, is individual; different students are motivated by different things. It is the teacher's job to know those motivations and adapt school to the student. Why is that still a radical notion in establishment circles? Why is it not a centerpiece of teacher preparation?

The struggle with the 2020 pandemic, which included the late winter or early spring closing of most schools in America, has laid bare the lack of motivation too prevalent for today's kids. In many reports of how schooling went under the rapid conversion to distance-learning, even those kids with regular online access repeatedly talked about being bored; some made themselves even hard to find. Some students volunteered that they hated school.

In a December 2019 edition online of the *New York Times*, the Learning Network published many quotes about the latest round of the Program for International Student Assessment (PISA) results from students. One student, Anders Olsen, from Hoggard High School in Wilmington, North Carolina, went straight to the solution:

> The answer to solving the American education crisis is simple. We need to put education back in the hands of the teachers. The politicians and the government need to step back and let the people who actually know what they are doing and have spent a lifetime doing it decide how to teach. We wouldn't let a lawyer perform heart surgery or construction workers do our taxes, so why let the people who win popularity contests run our education systems?

I could stop right there. Because Olsen said it all. He's probably never heard of the teacher-powered schools movement, but he understands the fundamental problem and the obvious solution.

In too many schools today, the curriculum is like being on a bus, the whole class taking a long tour. Someone else has determined the destinations. But you, as a student, might look out the window and see something interesting.

You are tempted to say, "Hey, look at that. Let's stop and explore it." But those in charge say, "We have to keep on our schedule. No time to stop."

The difference when schools are actually focused on students is that students are, sometime individually, driving that bus. And the teachers, more like coaches (usually called advisors in teacher-powered schools), may be offering commentary as the bus passes through interesting territory. But the students, along with the teacher's advice, decide what to pay attention to, when to stop and explore, and how long it takes to get to some destination.

Most schooling, sad to say, is organized like the first bus. Schools run by teachers, teacher-powered schools, are not. They are more like the second bus, because they have to be. There simply is no other way to be student-centered; no other path to personalization than through student motivation for learning.

So the policy question is why do students have to fit the system? Why do we score by proficiency a student's capacity to conform to what is expected? Why do not we expect the system to fit the students?

That is what teachers do once they are in charge, almost always. They get students engaged, motivated to learn. That is the essential difference. Again, Frymier had it right. His way of describing motivation is timeless: "If the kids want to learn, you can't stop them. If they don't you can't make 'em."

Do teachers have to be totally in charge of a school for learning to be student-centered, for young people to be motivated to learn? No. But teachers need considerably more influence over the learning program than most have today.

Teachers, back when most schools were small and had just one room, ran the whole show. Peer teaching was common; students who turned out to be faster helped those who were slower. What we now think of as grades were all mixed, with older students helping with younger ones. It had limitations of course, but it worked. Teachers had more say and so did students.

These practices began increasingly to be regarded as primitive and too small by the late 19th century. And when elite university presidents and the Carnegie Foundation for the Advancement of Teaching decided to formalize age-grading and what became known as Carnegie Units in the early 20th century, the stage was set for what Americans would think of as *real school*.

From time to time, people organized efforts to take down this new structure. In the 1920s and 1930s, there emerged something called the Dalton Plan, and later what is now remembered as the Eight Year Study. Both were rebellions of a sort against the idea of "real school." The Dalton Plan, named for a Massachusetts town, was more flexible, more student-centered, and gained a lot of international attention. But it faded, as did much of the change in Denver, which was prominent in the Eight Year Study. Real school got sticky in the minds of most people.

It is worth recalling that there was much fundamentally right about those one-room schools. We messed all that up with layers of administrative bureaucracy, with well-meaning structures like age-grading to make it easier to sort students, with politicized school board elections, with notions about standards that led to standardization, and with ideas about evaluating students efficiently that distorted the curriculum and deadened the atmosphere that could have been animated with motivated learning.

The National Alliance of Public Charter Schools had set Jaime Casap for its 2020 conference. The conference itself, after the pandemic set in, was converted to an online webinar. But in an interview with Alliance staff a couple months in advance, Casap, who has the unusual title of chief education evangelist at Google, talked about the crying need for a "culture shift." Then in response to a question about what a student will need to be prepared for the next decade, Casap said, "A student who is a lifelong learner who continues to develop their problem-solving, collaboration, and critical thinking skills." Among the changes he would make in the system: "Give schools more autonomy." That would be a major culture shift for the education industry, still stuck in what retired Stanford University professor Larry Cuban calls the grammar of schooling, or the structures and rules that govern how things are done.

A decade ago, a major business organization in one of America's regions did an internal survey of senior human resource officers in dozens of corporate headquarter companies, asking them what employers would be looking for as a hiring squeeze loomed. The results were never published, but the staffer was willing to disclose that the profile of responses read like the mission statement of most liberal arts colleges. They were saying, we can teach them the work we do, but we will try to avoid hiring people who are not *educated*.

Survey respondents used terms familiar to every liberal arts college: *collaboration*, *teamwork*, *problem solving*, *critical thinking*, *good judgment*. When Erika Hagberg, who at this writing is director of Global Sales for Google, was interviewed by the *Washington Post* last January, she was quick to credit her liberal arts preparation. I'm a better thinker, she said, as she observed the incredible pace of everything digitized. Hagberg is typical, saying what many others have said.

Which takes the focus to whether many teachers want more authority and what they might do with it. Teacher-powered schools may not be new, but they seem so when compared with dominant norms. Exploring the teacher-powered option is what this book is about. *Option* is an intentional term; not every teacher and not every school needs to change. But some want to change.

Still the belief persists that most teachers do not want this option. It yet seems normal to think that teachers prefer to work alone and that they are content to be the workers in a rather regimented industry.

Scott Widmeyer blew these assumptions away in 2013 when he conducted a national survey for EE. He found that most teachers had no idea that calling the shots in a school was a professional option. Teachers supported the idea and parents even more. Widmeyer's survey research was a major turning point for teachers interested in having more control over their work. (More on this in later chapters.)

Chapter 1 starts with reflections from a career teacher and then focuses on a vision for a better system than the one we know so well. And while that chapter will seem to focus a lot of attention on what happens with teachers, what happens to students matters most. When this works, it is obvious. It shows. You can almost feel it when you wander around the school. The students and the teachers have a different attitude than most people expect to find at school.

What is that difference? Probably mostly *motivation*. Some call this engagement. Regardless of what the terms are, the teachers have it. They would not be working in such a school without being motivated to be there. And the students, whether they are there by choice or by assignment, discover quickly that they are important individuals in this scheme, not just one of many. Their personal interests and aptitudes are relevant. The pace at which they learn things gets respect, as does the way they learn best.

Chapter 2 lays out the critical importance of autonomy. *Autonomy* is an easy word to use; it can mean many things. But in this context it means having real authority over what matters for student and school success. And rather than leave that notion vague, those tracking this growing movement have made a list of critical autonomies. To gain designation as a teacher-powered school, you have to demonstrate that the teacher team at that school has all or some of at least four of fifteen identified autonomies. This chapter will explain why these autonomies matter, the first ten of which came from the observations made by the authors of *Trusting Teachers with School Success*. Five more would be eventually added by the EE team, as they understood more about what autonomies enabled teachers to have real authority over their work.

Also, this chapter will radically simplify the deal the public has with teachers, where that deal came from, and how it has changed over the years.

The next chapter, chapter 3, describes the movement of teacher-powered schools—where it came from, how and why it is growing, and what makes it different from what most people think of as real school. Teacher-powered schools may have started as a research project, but then became an initiative, and then a network, and now looks more like a national movement. As the reader will find quickly enough, this proposition rests on the will of parents and other constituents to trust what teachers think and what they will do with real authority.

When Ed Dirkswager, who spent his career in other fields, such as health care and state and local government, came out with the edited book *Teachers as Owners* in 2002, this idea still seemed like a radical departure—something few people understood. The turning point came in 2013 when he helped Kim Farris-Berg with *Trusting Teachers with School Success,* a book that sparked the nascent movement and told compelling stories of how schools we now think of as teacher-powered were fundamentally different kinds of organizations. These schools shared many of the characteristics people associate with high-performing organizations. From the work of Farris-Berg on, teacher-powered started to look like a lasting movement.

Now people ask: will teachers—if they get more authority—only make life better for themselves? Or, if some get more autonomy over their work, will they use the authority to nudge schooling toward joining the club of self-improving organizations, capable of changing and adapting the way other successful organizations do? Chapter 3 will also provide numbers as to how many such schools are known today, where they are, and what variations are known within the model of teachers being in charge. And whether even so-called average people can make a noticeable difference in results.

The next chapter, chapter 4, imagines the possibility that the movement, already growing every year, might take off, become bigger, faster. Laying out the six strategies for making this happen—most of which cost money, adding up to at least a few millions a year. This nation invests huge sums in many things. The amount of funding that might accelerate a teacher-powered future is modest by comparison. Actually, in most communities, assistance of a few thousand dollars could free up teams of teachers to plan for taking over a school or starting a new one. Money is not the central issue, but some money might help.

Then, Chapter 5 consciously struggles with obstacles to more rapid growth. Those obstacles are like rocks in the road. You can still get there but the ride may be rough. This chapter will ask whether getting bigger too fast exposes the movement to distortion of mission at best, or even something like a takeover by powerful interests. The biggest rock in the road though may be what technology now makes possible—something close to total by-pass of the system as we know it. The 2020 pandemic, among its many consequences, may actually accelerate this possibility.

Many students have discovered what it is like to be independent learners. Many, despite the dominant system's failure to adapt to technological change, proved that they were already the digital natives some observers said they were. Maybe today's students do not know the best software and apps for learning, but they do know more about technology and its uses than any previous generation. For some students, it became clear that academics could be as flexible as athletics; you could be classified by how fast you learn and how good you become, not how old you are or what grade adults have put you in.

Chapter 6 is devoted to the dilemma about teacher unions. If demand for this option grows, what will the unions say? Most books in recent years paint these unions as the problem, an obstacle, perhaps even the enemy of change and progress. Unions certainly throw up a lot of barriers and it is tempting always to put them in the barrier category. As the 2020 political season gets underway, teachers unions seem to be waging an active campaign against any competitors, what Kerchner once called "trench warfare."

But it may be that unions are the key to scaling up an overdue change. They may be capable of mobilizing a mostly dormant army for this change. Unions need to change themselves. If they are the democratic organizations they say they are, will they not listen to this demand? This chapter will lay out the case for working with unions at the local, state and national levels.

For a long time, the most progressive elected heads and activists in local unions all over the country, met at least once a year as the Teacher Union Reform Network (TURN). Years later, the network is now emphasizing regional meetings. Joe Graba, who was always considered a "critical friend," believed that union officials were able to see how some union people succeeded in getting control of professional issues. Graba was a former Minnesota legislator, a former higher education executive, and, with Kolderie, a founder of EE.

Finally, the book in chapter 7 will arrive at conclusions. It will point to changes that could make schooling a self-improving system, help students find their form of intelligence and skill, and give teachers a shot at becoming a real profession. Offer teachers a new deal. Many might take it. The nation would be the winner.

Chapter 1

Imagine a Different School
Teaching as a Real Profession

REFLECTIONS OF A RETIRED TEACHER

I always wanted to be a teacher. Especially once I figured out that veterinarians had to do a lot more than cuddle puppies. I grew up in Milwaukee and went to Milwaukee Public Schools (MPS). Not only did I have Milwaukee in my blood but since my father was the Executive Director with the American Federation of State County and Municipal Employees (AFSCME) union and my grandfather and great-grandfather had been union organizers, I had a consistently union view of the world. While I was working in schools, I was nearly always the union representative.

My experience, once I was a teacher, was mixed. I loved teaching, but I never felt like my administrators were in it for the kids or the professional growth of the staff. But I stuck with it because I loved the work with the students. When I was finally able to get into Victory School, I was thrilled. They had a history of respecting teachers as decision-makers. The school was IGE (Individually Guided Education) and a wonderful place for kids and staff. Then a new principal came, who, against the wishes of parents and teachers, changed the whole program. Some people suggested to us that we could start our own school. So our journey began.

I'd always wanted to create a school that would fit the needs of a diverse group of students and teachers. I wanted to be involved in creating systemic change for Milwaukee's kids from within MPS. The big breakthrough came when we heard about the Minnesota New Country School in Henderson, Minnesota, started in 1994. It was the late 90s now and the school was attracting grants and lots of visitors.

My dad and a couple of teachers went with me upon the suggestion of an MPS school board director. One visit was all it took. I thought, finally, maybe we can have the best of all worlds. We can start an "instrumentality" charter, which in Wisconsin means it's a charter within the district, staffed with all union members. We knew that could be limiting, but it meant we could gather teachers who also didn't want to walk away from the district.

The five-hour ride from Henderson back to Milwaukee was all talk about how we could create our new school, and use all union people. The union supported us and so did the school board. We organized a partnership of teachers and a group of committed parents. The district gave one wing in an old middle school building, but it was a start. And that's how IDEAL (Individualized Developmental Educational Approaches to Learning—named by my Mom) became the first teacher-led school in the Milwaukee district, actually anywhere in Wisconsin.

One huge factor in our ability to create these schools was that the former principal of a middle school, Bill Andrekopolous, became superintendent and he supported and encouraged us throughout the process. He understood our frustration with not being able to control our professional destiny. He knew we wanted and believed we could handle real autonomy, actual ownership, and that we'd feel and be fully accountable.

The name of the school was IDEAL, but a lot of conditions were not. We had to scrounge for necessary materials for that first year, sometimes even dumpster diving to recapture things thrown away by other schools. But here's what made it work: we were a real community; the students and the parents were truly involved. It was a completely different thing than most of us had known. The same things happened when I was involved in opening high schools using the grant money that came into the district from the Bill and Melinda Gates Foundation. High school students spent time getting classrooms ready, recruiting, and even worked on the school's by-laws along with the staff. Imagine that—teenagers in school because they wanted to be. We often had to send them home so we could leave and feed our children and pets!

We were very lucky to be able to travel, often with the help of Education Evolving, with students and teachers to visit other places and speak to groups, as we did in Washington D.C. to the American Federation of Teachers, Newark, Philadelphia, Seattle, Reno and other cities in Wisconsin. Our staff and students were great ambassadors to tell the story of how teachers in charge of a school worked better for all involved.

Then a new superintendent came. He was all about finances, not people. He talked about "economies of scale," and thought any school with fewer than 2000 students wasn't fiscally responsible. Sameness was the slogan. He'd say, "If I go to Burger King in Boston and in Taiwan, I should be able to buy the exact same burger." Everyone was required to use the same calendars, schedules, report cards, text books. The differences we fought for were dissolving. If test scores weren't good enough, there was blame, even though many of our high school students who fell below the expected level had dropped out before, only returning because ours was a different kind of school. Those students showed significant gains the longer they stayed in our high schools.

At about the same time, the union guard changed too. The new people were not as enthusiastic about the Memoranda of Understandings we had. They were not as willing to push back against a central office never fond of our being run by teachers, not having someone they could identify as the principal. And there had always been skeptics out there, including our own union brothers and sisters, people who simply did not believe that teachers could be in charge of a school.

Today there are only two schools left in the district that are what is now called "teacher-led." Only two. The last one I helped open—and we had about a dozen at the peak—was SUPAR (School for Urban Planning and Architecture), which opened in the fall of 2007. When it closed due to the superintendent's new budget requirements, it felt like I was losing a child.

I am now retired, but I am inspired and encouraged to see this movement growing all across the country. My message to all involved is "fight the good fight."

Cris Parr
Milwaukee, Wisconsin

Imagine teachers excited about the upcoming school year, eager to see students again. Imagine students, rather than dreading the end of a too-short summer, taking their now constant love of learning back into a schooling environment, telling their parents, even their friends, that being in school makes them come alive. That their teachers—more like coaches—are helping them plow their own path through the wilderness of knowledge to find what they like most and do best.

They can count on their teachers being there, since in their school the retention rate is close to 100 percent. Those kids will do well on mandatory testing, but that is never taught. They will graduate and do well in college, even if that institution groans with tradition and confronts them with too much they already know; they will handle it as they will with every new chapter of life.

Now many seasoned observers would say that the foregoing scenario was hopelessly romanticized. But school does not have to be something students dread. Or merely endure until it is over. Parr's story above may be discouraging, because it shows so well how difficult it is to start and sustain a new kind of school in an established district.

But what makes the Parrs of this world optimistic is the small but steadily growing movement of teachers fully in charge of schools. And how different these schools turn out to be. By the end of 2019, EE had designated some 150 schools in 20 different states of the United States as being teacher-powered.

Teacher-powered became the name and the slogan (www.teacherpowered.org). The name was not chosen lightly, but no one pretends it is ideal either. It was chosen by the team that had the responsibility to foster and nurture the prospective movement. What had been an initiative, then a network, could become a movement. But these schools needed a name.

And after the Widmeyer survey research in 2013, on top of the Public Agenda results in 2003 (which showed that teachers in this Yankelovich-conducted survey were ready—at least 58 percent of them—to join schools run by teachers, even if it meant shifting to a chartered school, a big move for some of them), there is now little question about the level of interest of teachers in being in charge of what matters in schools. The 2013 results showed major interest by teachers in having more authority and that sentiment was supported by even more parents. But, the problem was, as Widmeyer found, most people, including teachers, had no idea this was a professional option (more on this survey later).

For all its limitations "teacher-powered" is not yet damaged as most labels are. "Teacher leadership," as one example, is burdened with multiple meanings at the least and maybe so distorted as to be useless; if teachers have any say in instructional matters, some schools claim teacher leadership.

In addition to having a national organization now tracking and nurturing the movement, three national conferences have brought teachers together to share their experiences and learn from each other. These conferences, held first in Minneapolis in 2015 and then in Los Angeles (2017) and Boston (2018), consistently sell to full capacity registration. They turn out to be highly unusual mixtures of teachers from districts and charters, from union settings and nonunion settings.

Whatever controversies may divide educators over districts and chartering and between union affiliations, they do not show up much at these conferences. The talk is mostly about how to solve problems, how to motivate kids, how to run the school.

Anyone observing these teachers will start to wonder why teaching is different from the other occupations considered professions? Not all law firms are the same but the general model is one of partnership. The same is true of most consulting firms, accounting firms, and all other professional organizations.

Imagine a Different School

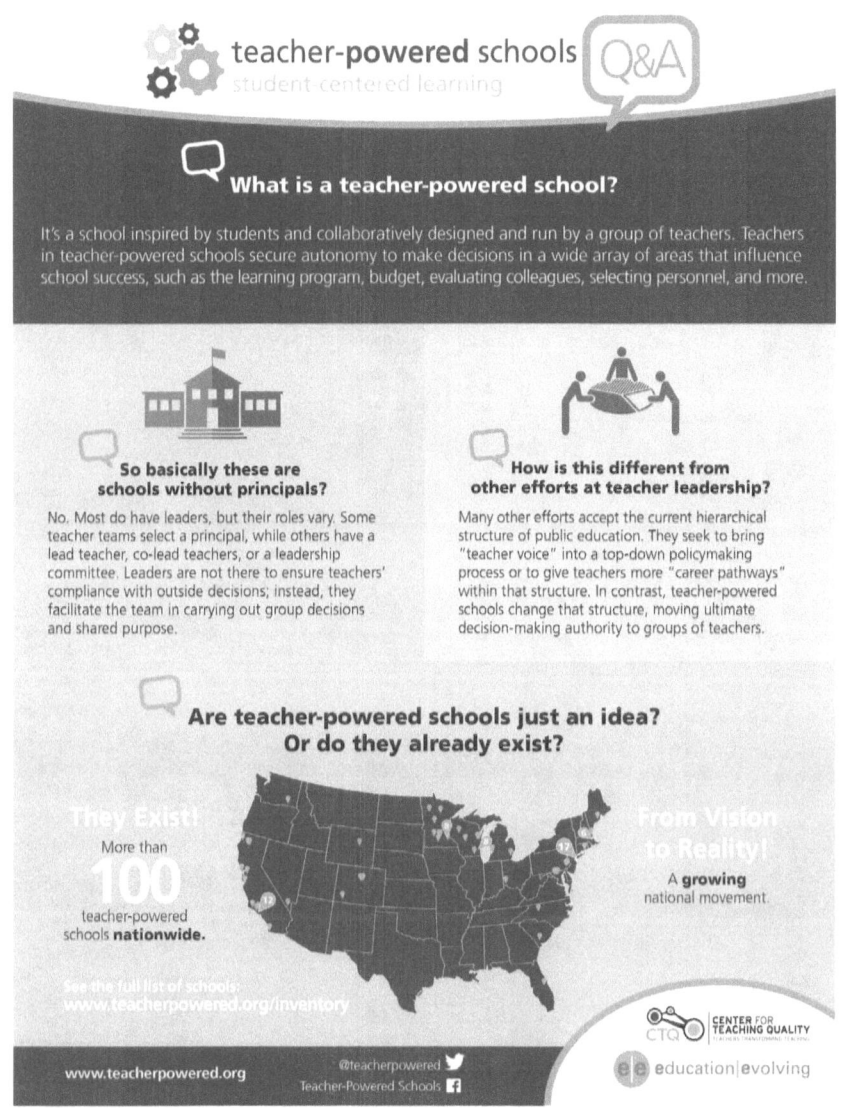

Figure 1.1 **Teacher Leadership.** *Teacher-Powered Schools.*

Why not teaching? Why is it stuck in a management—labor model that assumes a boss and a worker? Figure 1.1 illustrates both what constitutes a teacher-powered school and the level of support this idea already enjoys.

Interviews with dozens of these teachers—all of whom have taken some level of responsibility for the whole school—have taken on a pattern that is predictable. The first thing most say is they figured out there was work none

Figure 1.1 (Continued).

of them wanted to do or felt competent or prepared to do. So, they hired others to do that work. Or they learned the skills themselves. They called these staff by many titles, the most prominent of which was "principal." The difference: the principal reported to the teachers.

Most teacher-powered schools have principals, though in many cases, those principals also do some of the teaching.

After that point in the interview, most teachers are eager to persuade whoever's asking about their experience that being in charge of the school is a lot more work. At least more work than they had experienced just teaching in a traditional classroom. They used the term *burn-out*; some find themselves residents at its edge. You would imagine them saying next that there is no way they would ever accept responsibility for a whole school. As Mary Cathryn Ricker, a former executive vice president of the American Federation of Teachers and now the commissioner of education for Minnesota put it, "It's what we've been conditioned to think; we'll be told what to do. There is lots of unlearning to do. And many teachers just want to close the door and do their job. Nothing else."

And just when an interviewer thinks that is the whole story they shift to describing what is the most satisfying professional experience they have ever known.

They are all full of enthusiasm for the kind of collaboration they are going through—even when it proves tough, when problems seem insoluble. *Collaboration*—a word for working together rather than separately, fellowship among colleagues, trying out things with others—seems to be the glue that sticks in these schools. The teachers are eager to tell stories about students, particularly those the system seems to have given up on, who show every promise of doing well.

And critically, when asked about accountability, they all—really, all of them—say almost the same thing. That once they knew they were really in charge of what mattered for student and school success, they felt accountable. Fully. Completely. There was no one else to blame for poor results. And for most, this did not seem like a burden; more like a challenge, something to live up to.

Once they accepted accountability, these teachers figured out some way to make the learning experience student-centered. Everyone has known for a long time that kids today are not only different from each other but are different from every previous generation of students. To organize school as though they were all alike would be absurd. That it is still the norm in many American schools does not make the practice less ridiculous, but more.

Putting students at the center of learning has been the subject of conferences for decades. Educators attend, applaud key speakers, discuss the concept in small groups, and sometimes even promise to make this approach their own. Then, they return home and repeat the methodologies that are so familiar. Sometimes they have no choice. Many say they are told what to do, when to do it, and how to carry it out.

That is apparently why many teachers quit, at least the job if not the whole career. But not if they find a school that encourages them to be full professionals, to learn from their experiences, and to look forward to a satisfying career.

"Satisfying" may mean more than just having a good job, starting a promising career. Most teachers readily declare that school is primarily for students. That they are the main reason for all this fuss. That their motivation, their learning, their success—that is what really matters. And that principle lies at the heart of why teachers should be in charge of what matters.

In fact, some teachers in teacher-powered schools will immediately correct a visitor who focuses too much on the teachers. It is really about the students. When this author entered the Urban Assembly School for Green Careers (UAGC) in New York city and explained the premise of the book about the teacher-powered movement, Chris Sedatis, one of the teachers, immediately said, "Well, I would take issue with the premise. This is a student-centered school. The teachers just make that happen." Well said. The teachers are clearly partners in the design of the learning, many will say. It becomes quickly clear that students, their interests, their inclinations, are at the center of how the school is organized. That does not mean students do not have to measure up, meet standards. But these schools do seem to have a way of acknowledging the differences among students and giving those differences some room to explore and grow.

In one class at UAGC, students were taking turns presenting ideas they wanted to pursue. Various teachers floated in and out of the class, took their turns at asking questions or offering suggestions to the students. It was clear that the students were in charge of their own learning but that adults were helping.

And that is what is different about schools where teachers are in charge of a school's learning program: there is an atmospheric difference that is hard to describe. But it is there. Even a visitor detects the enthusiasm. The students actually want to be there. One teacher who was a pioneer in the movement had been a principal in a traditional school. She said, "I used to have to persuade kids to come to school. How I have to persuade them to leave." Capturing that spirit is what this movement is about.

Chapter 2

Teachers Can Do It
Autonomy Is the Key

Ted Sanders was in 2001 the relatively new chief executive of the Education Commission of the States, a national education organization. Sitting behind his big desk at headquarters, he pondered the question. He had been asked by two visitors what he thought of giving teachers real control over what mattered in school. After a long pause, he said, succinctly, he would never permit that. Why? Well, recalling his former days as a school district superintendent, he said that if he consented to such an arrangement, he would lose no matter what happened: in other words, if the teachers did well, he wouldn't get the credit; if the whole thing flopped, he would get all the blame. So why do it?

Just about the same response came from the first emergency financial manager of the Detroit Public Schools, Robert Bobb, in 2010. He was in a room with a half-dozen teachers, activists in the Detroit teachers' union, who essentially said they would be willing to take over a few of the worst performing schools in the district. And they said they knew many other teachers prepared to do the same thing. (They knew, because each of them had been at a meeting at the Traffic Jam and Snug—an improbably named restaurant near Wayne State University, called to check support for the idea.) The teachers left the meeting with Bobb disappointed. They returned to their posts, doing the best they could, while being told what to do and when to do it almost every day. Bobb went on hiring outside consultants, closing failing schools, and seeing the district deficit, already in the hundreds of millions of dollars, grow even larger.

The story gets repeated over and over: districts with overdue needs for improvement in results predictably decline to give teachers any real authority over the school.

Put simply, the deal the United States had with teachers for about a century was: we are not going to give you any real authority, but we are also not going to hold you ultimately accountable. Do a good job? Great. Just do the minimum to get by; you will still have a job. Still get the same pay.

When No Child Left Behind (NCLB) passed in 2001, no one said so explicitly, but the effort was on to change the deal—unilaterally. Still, the public was not offering teachers any increase in real control over their work, not offering a deal to become a full professional. But what was changing was accountability. Now, teachers would be evaluated by how well students did, on a standardized test. Yes, the same test for every child, regardless of background or aptitude for test-taking. In essence, you (the teacher) still do not have authority, but we are going to hold you accountable.

No surprise then when teachers reported they were demoralized, felt indicted, blamed. No surprise that teachers unions, that exist to represent the interest of teachers, fought back. Why would they not? It was a raw deal, a bad bargain, an arrangement no real professional would accept.

Can anyone imagine attorneys or accountants or architects taking such a deal? In just about every profession, if you have the credentials, you essentially control your professional work. Is that work evaluated? Sure. Criticism? Yes, it comes with the job. But you have a serious say in anything that matters for your clients and the firm's success. That has not been true in elementary and secondary education since the one-room schoolhouse gave way to scale and modernity.

With the passage of the Every Student Succeeds Act (ESSA) in 2015, the successor to NCLB stipulated that much of the power for evaluation would revert back to the states, where education is actually in constitutions (and not in any federal founding documents). But the mindset of teachers as pawns, as just cogs in a big machine, persists.

THE MINDSET BARRIER

Graba, the longtime educator mentioned before who also was once the chair of the House K–12 Education Finance Committee of the Minnesota Legislature, put it this way in a 2003 conversation with Kolderie, with whom he founded the network known as EE:

> I talk a lot to boards and superintendents and it is clear they just cannot believe teachers can do this. They are astounded at the thought of teachers running a school. The public probably still does not really believe teachers are professionals. What's reassuring to me about the teacher-owner models I've seen is that teachers change their behavior radically when they own the operation. It is a lot of work. But they spend almost no time in the coffee room complaining about the administration and the board. Decisions get made and they do not argue afterward. Their energy is redirected in a very positive way.

Also, in my opinion, this is the best way to provide teacher leadership. I despair at trying to find enough principals committed to a strong teacher role in the school. We are the only professional institution to combine administrative and professional leadership in a single organizational position. Any law firm of any size has an administrator; any medical clinic does. The professionals hire that administrator. The administrator *never* hires the professionals. The two roles are incompatible. Very few people have the capacity to do justice to both roles. A principal gets selected by the people above, and what matters most to the people above is good, smooth administration.

Some people, like Nora Whalen, one of the longtime lead teachers at Saint Paul-based, teacher-powered Avalon School, where teachers have organized to do almost everything, says it bluntly, "People just get scared about the amount of work."

There are many theories about this mindset barrier. One that is quite credible is that the Council of Great City Schools started something that took hold and has been slow to change. People with long memories say that the Council had commissioned a study a generation back that found urban districts pursuing a way-too-wide range of approaches to learning; so the solution was to standardize what teachers did. The result for many urban districts was "managed instruction" (sometimes called "focused instruction"), which infuriated many teachers who thought of themselves as in charge at least of their classrooms. One high school teacher told anyone who would listen that the scripts were so specific, she could turn the whole business over to the students. She was no longer needed. And she eventually quit the career.

Regardless of provenance, that mindset barrier persists. It shows up directly and subtly in conversations with all kinds of people. People of all kinds of backgrounds and professional expertise when asked about teachers being in charge of school look and sound perplexed. Remember, most people are quite familiar with how other industries are structured. They tend to admire (mostly) what has happened in digital technology. They point to competition, to the open atmosphere that expects, sometimes even invites an entrepreneurial move. They will quote Steve Jobs, the late founder of Apple, as saying, "People don't know what they want until we give it to them."

But when it comes to school, their minds collapse into the conditioning that we are permanently bound to the management and labor model that has been the norm for about a hundred years in the United States.

Even when people concede that industries that get better tend to become self-improving, they do not apply that to education; they persist in this mindset even when they see that professionals working in other industries have the freedom, sometimes strong encouragement, to try things. To fail. To learn from what does not work well. Even then, most people who start out unfamiliar with this nascent movement, just cannot believe that teachers can be in charge of schools.

Of course, this impulse does not resonate with every teacher. But this divide over preference for real influence shows up in any industry. There are people who want to control their work and many others who clearly prefer to do whatever work they are assigned. No successful industry gets that way by changing everyone or everything at once. But what is the argument for stopping those who want to be full professionals and fully control their work? What's wrong with having the option? That is what the system seems to oppose, seems to work against.

The last refuge of objectors is to cite conventional statistics claiming the nation has been drawing most teachers from the lower quartiles of the college-going population for more than a generation. Their conclusion: most teachers are average people.

When people say "average," they seem to imply it is below some sort of standard. It is very difficult to find any confirming data for this contention, yet it persists and is often repeated. And certainly, the proliferation of for-profit schools of education with their sometimes lower bar for entry feeds this narrative.

But even stipulating this condition as a fact, what difference does that actually make? George Eastman was considered average. So was Charles Goodyear. And especially the Wright Brothers—all considered average people, maybe even on their way to mediocre lives. Who would have guessed that two brothers running a bicycle shop in Ohio would figure out the key to getting a heavier-than-air craft off the ground? But it was not their field, actually, so they did not know they could not do it.

In *Engineers of Victory*, Yale historian Paul Kennedy argues that the Allies prevailed in World War II because the big problems were solved by people whose names you will never know.

The people cited by Kennedy were knowledgeable but not famous; they were not the people in charge of major enterprises, but people close to the action. They figured out everything from miniaturizing radar to retrofitting fighter planes with longer-range engines. In Kennedy's terms, the nation had adopted a "culture of encouragement," so that people in a position to know what they were doing felt free to try new and different solutions. And if something did not work, they could try again. Until it worked.

That is the point—having a culture that emphasizes trying things, that promotes collaboration rather than going it alone, that encourages people to take risks rather than avoid trouble and criticism.

Getting better results from school is certainly a different challenge than World War II. But that challenge may require the same culture of encouragement, the same freedom to try things, and trusting those who are close to the action. In this case, the teachers.

Actually, in the schooling world, autonomy may be better understood by coaches. They are measured with regularity by results. But legendary hockey coach Herb Brooks never gave out a textbook to anyone. And no one told him *how* to coach. He felt all the accountability any professional could. And so did every member of the team.

In that sense, athletics is ahead of the rest of schooling. As Herb Childress pointed out in his essay, "Seventeen Reasons Why Football Is Better Than High School," in team sports participants spend as much time as they need to get better. And they have to, because the team is on the line at least once a week. And they have to click, work together, pull hard to get good results. When does that happen inside the rest of school, Childress asks? (And Childress admits, by the way, that he actually hates football. But the comparison is provocative.)

Most teachers who feel real autonomy say they want to extend more flexibility to students. Lincoln Bacal, who is a senior at Venture Academy in Minneapolis, put it this way: "I'd go to the next step—give some real responsibility to students. They're looking to experience the real world, not just sit in classrooms and be told things." Bacal understands the difference between an encouraging environment and one where the prime people get ignored.

One rather unusual superintendent found the same thing when he started working toward changing the climate, the working model of an entire district. It took four or five years, the first ones largely consumed with persuading teachers that distributing leadership (a fancy term for introducing serious professional autonomy for teachers) was real, not the usual fabricated happy-talk that has made cynics of so many teachers.

In his conservative-leaning, exurban district, Jay Haugen, always more inclined to seek forgiveness than permission, managed to get just about everyone in that district tuned into learning. He was aiming to affect the culture around school, as much as possible. That starts with spreading autonomy.

Haugen was superintendent in an area that had been a very small farming community. Now the district gets a regular flow of visitors. But most say, even after hearing the story, "This is wonderful but we can't do this. We could never give this kind of authority to our staff." Haugen just shakes his head.

"We'd give those who were willing all the 'agency' they could handle," Haugen would say. "Then others would see that and say, 'Why do they get to do that?' and we'd remind them that anyone can do it." It took a while, several years, but teachers, students, even community members in that district now understand what autonomy really means.

Haugen's district is not considered teacher-powered, but it is close. Teachers have been given something close to the autonomy enjoyed in teacher-powered schools, at least control over how the learning program is conducted. That is the key and experiencing that control obliterates the old mindset.

Ingersoll has been an academic at a university for a long time, but he's encountered this same mindset objection about authority over and over. "It's a form of blindness," he says, "and it is particularly ironic for those who have lots of voice in their work but don't see it for others." The idea, he says, is so persistent, so ingrained, that there must be a boss in every situation.

The students get the change fast. And it shows. Every known school in the inventory of teacher-powered schools, has some system for greater autonomy of students, something not present in schools where teachers feel powerless themselves. So, just maybe, autonomy is not only the *sine qua non* of a truly teacher-powered school arrangement, but it is also the key to getting students to experience the responsibility that only comes from having the freedom to explore, to fail, to find what works.

No one spelled this out better than Dee Thomas, a former principal in a traditional high school, who was part of the early group of teachers in the early years of Minnesota New Country School (MNCS) in rural Henderson, Minnesota. Thomas had the assignment of speaking at the annual event West Virginia puts on to take stock of where the state is and lay out its aspirations for the future.

Thomas told the assembled group a story of a new student at MNCS, often expelled from other schools, nearly a victim of suicide, on what most people considered her last chance in school. Thomas said the girl showed little interest; after all, it was just another school. So Thomas asked her: "What are you interested in?" That's all she asked. At first, the young person didn't really believe the teacher cared about the answer. But finally she said, "Well, I love motorcycles."

So what did Dee Thomas do? (And this is what real autonomy, not "fauxtonomy," looks like). She—and the student—designed the entire school year experience around building a motorcycle. In the process, the student learned a lot of physics, math, certainly mechanics, energy dynamics, plus learning to explain her work at MNCS's regular gathering of parents and community people.

Did she learn everything the state standards contemplated? Actually, she might have. But she certainly discovered the joy of learning, of exploring something, the pride in achievement. She built a motorcycle and could explain what she did. She could make anyone interested in the subject.

And, Thomas reports, this woman is still alive. She is a productive citizen, a success with her work and life. And that West Virginia audience—about half of them were in tears as Thomas finished her story.

This episode that Dee Thomas recalls illustrated well what nearly every teacher does with professional autonomy—put students at the center of what the school is about. She was focused, as most teacher-powered schools are, on everything that makes that student a different human being. That is the process that makes the system self-improving.

INSTITUTIONAL RESISTANCE

Frank Coyne, one of the founding teachers of the Green School in Denver, was speaking to a policy conference gathered in Denver in the summer of 2019. It was a conference sponsored by the School of Public Affairs of the University of Colorado at Denver. Coyne's role was to describe his experience with Colorado's Innovation Schools law. The law, sponsored by then Colorado state senator Peter Groff, passed in the Colorado legislature in 2008. Its aim was to introduce more innovative pathways for better student outcomes—something almost no one could be against.

The Green School got started as an "innovation school." As David Osborne reported in his book about *Reinventing America's Schools*, Green School stands out among the schools with that designation, largely because it gets consistently high academic marks. It does that largely through projects; students discovered, Osborne wrote, that they could save a million gallons of water in the school's garden each year, just by using drip lines and good sense about when to water. The theme of the whole school is environmental sustainability; the community sees this at the school's farm stand every week.

The law that passed in Colorado gave schools greater rights to control their staffing, their budgets, their schedules, and any operations that need to be better aligned with the schools approach to learning. The Green School is organized as a teacher partnership, with three teachers (who still teach some) sharing the duties of managing the school. (Any one of the thirty-two other teachers, according to Osborne's book, can apply to join the management team.) Again, the effort was mostly about leveling the field with the growing charter sector, even though innovation schools would not have as much real autonomy as charters. But the autonomy idea was infectious, according to Coyne.

Coyne told the group that while the state was far-sighted in opening up the sector, even districts as progressive as Denver's still wanted to control things. Coyne said the law was very specific and he talked about the autonomies that, once the school was approved, they should have.

But the Denver district was not going along. Superintendent Tom Boasberg told Coyne, when confronted about the law, "You just don't want a boss."

Eventually, as Coyne told the group, he got nearly all of his colleagues who represented the Innovation Schools to join him in a major meeting at the central office. The law was clear; the district was waffling. The group demanded the autonomies, in writing, that the law stipulated. They got them. Coyne said as he finished the story, almost inaudibly, that the struggle was not over.

As Amy Junge, who directs EE's national network of teacher-powered schools, is quick to remind anyone, "It is never over." Schools that choose to be different are always targets for people who want to keep everything the same.

Emily Langhorne, formerly of the Progressive Policy Institute, tells the sad story of what happened in the Los Angeles Unified School District. The schools known as pilot schools started there, as they did in Boston, as a means of creating serious competition with emerging charter schools. Most pilot schools had real autonomy. And that was valued and protected by then superintendent John Deasy, said Langhorne.

But when Deasy left, his successor reverted to more traditional structures. "And there was nothing they could do about it," she said. The entire district is stumbling toward a "portfolio" status, having several kinds of schools and mixed governance. Its future as a district operation is uncertain.

In his 2017 book, Osborne wrote that there are about fifty pilot schools in Los Angeles (out of a total of more than a 1000), which sprang from the Boston example. The teachers are still district employees, still represented by the union, but they have to vote on an elect-to-work agreement that gets outside the union contract in areas such as work hours.

The pilot schools seem to still have more flexibility and their academic progress is exceeded only by the independent charters, according to Osborne. Each of these schools has an elected governing council, which includes the principals, some teachers, parents and students. Several of these boards ceded authority to the teacher teams, making them effectively, according to Junge, teacher-powered.

Sometimes, autonomy erupts even in a traditional school. In the early years of this century, Ananth Pai, born in Mumbai, India, and finding himself in Saint Paul, Minnesota, decided to end his successful career in the printing industry and get credentials to become a teacher. Though he found teacher preparation to be largely boring and sometimes irrelevant, he got his degree and found a job in 2007, a third-grade assignment in a suburban public school designated as International Baccalaureate.

His first weeks felt like months. He was doing exactly what he was trained to do and what the school's curriculum guide suggested. Nothing was working. The kids were not responding. He told his wife if work did not get better, he had made a mistake. He would quit.

To make matters worse, he had looked at proficiency scores for all the kids assigned to his third-grade classroom. Predictably, they were all over the range—some very low, others higher. How would he teach to this kind of range?

Then Pai had an idea: ask what the students were interested in. His own kids had answers. So did others. One of them was video games.

Pai began a slow, methodical investigation of what software and games were out there that kids liked but also had educational value. As he found some, those were introduced into his classroom work. The kids changed. They seemed to love working with games, responding to software.

The school would not buy what Pai needed so he raised money, managing to get matching funds from his wife's employer. When he needed more, he funded acquisitions himself.

Later, as most of the day was devoted to learning using computers and video games, a visitor—and there were many—might see a table of kids with laptops equipped with math problem software. The students who mastered the drills faster reached out to help the slower ones. Pai would say this was not because he told them to do that (though he had refrained from interfering with what he observed).

Over in one corner of the room, about ten kids were playing (or working, depending on your definition of the experience) with Nintendo DS devices. The main character was always getting into some predicament, and to resolve his problems, he required tools. And those tools were only accessible by naming and spelling them correctly.

As just one example of learning, every couple of weeks, using paper and pencils, Pai would ask students to write down (and spell correctly) all the new words they thought they had learned. The vocabulary results were amazing, and not only for the kids at the upper end of beginning proficiency.

One might think the school, though it was a traditional public school, that at least the principal, would be pleased. Not so. The principal was constantly critical, telling Pai once that he was embarrassing the other teachers. Notably, Pai was not in a teacher-powered school, where his experience would have been very different.

Meanwhile, Pai would get calls from parents with a new worry. Their kids were continuing their schoolwork at home. Without being told to. It was not assigned homework. But by the end of the year parents were more concerned about how kids would react to the next grade if they found themselves back in the traditionally structured class.

A ten-year-old student in Mr. Pai's classroom, Cordell Steiner, made a TEDx talk in 2014, in which he exclaimed that Pai's classroom "rocked," because learning had been "individualized," that it was no longer necessary to teach to the average. Steiner told the audience that "failure was an awesome experience," that he and all the students were learning from failure.

But did this form of learning and the individualization it hinged on spread or scale? No. Pai would later say, "I could not be more stunned by the bureaucratic apathy."

It may not be apathy but just institutional resistance, the unvarying tendency of any mature organization to sweep any change back into its standard business model, into the culture of what worked for so long.

What Pai was doing with video games is not an argument for replication. But it is an object lesson about the system, about its need to have everyone on the same page every day in every school. And once again, it shows how difficult it is to do anything new or different in a system that prizes uniformity.

What frustrates so many who see a better way may be the unconscious but real drive to be seen as doing the right thing, to be "legitimate." That at least was the conclusion that James (known better as Torch) Lytle came to while still doing turnarounds in the Philadelphia district before his highly successful stint as superintendent in the troubled Trenton (NJ) district. Many times an author, especially once he became a professor at the University of Pennsylvania, Lytle's comments on practice were always memorable. None more so than his observation early in his career, that the pressures felt by urban districts particularly "to be 'legitimate institutions' so preoccupy the board and central office that they are unable to be responsive to their clients—because to do so they would need to reconfigure their ways of delivering services so radically they would no longer be considered 'legitimate' school districts."

INTIMATIONS OF TEACHER POWER

Before there were schools run by teachers, there were hints, pressure points, instances of schools getting more autonomy. Not all these schools would be designated as teacher-powered today, but they show the significance of tasting autonomy. Here are a few examples.

Edmonton

One from the mid-1970s was Edmonton, Alberta, in Canada. There an educator who had served the district as a teacher, principal, and an assistant in the superintendent's office became superintendent in 1973, and based on many years of feeling the effects of centralization, he became intensely committed to the opposite. He became the highly regarded champion of site-based management at the time.

Over Michael Strembitsky's tenure, most of the schools in the Edmonton public schools got real autonomy over just about everything that mattered, including most of the school budget. Results were good. People seemed more satisfied. Parents were pleased. Students did well. The superintendent, once he retired, became an international salesman for school autonomy. But the model never spread.

Milwaukee

Then Milwaukee's story unfolded. It's a story about a thirty-eight-year veteran of Milwaukee schools, fourteen spent as a principal, who one day in 2002 found himself in charge of the entire district. When Bill Andrekopolous became superintendent, there was already one school with no principal but what he did next was quite unusual.

Actually, Andrekopolous had a history of doing the unexpected. In 1999, when he was principal of Fritsche Middle School, he ruffled lots of feathers by packaging and sending back the district's standardized tests for students, saying they were not good enough for his students. Acts of rebellion toward the central office were rare enough. But then to be picked as superintendent?

In his new role, Andrekopolous was soon confronted with teachers who thought they could run a school, particularly in areas where the dominant student population did not do well, he said, "Why not?" Bill and Melinda Gates Foundation grants came along, aimed at creating a constellation of small schools, even high schools, and that helped to lubricate the specter of big change.

IDEAL in 2002 was the first school to emerge, under the inspired leadership of Cris Parr (whose story starts this chapter) and her father, John, who'd been an American Federation of State County and Municipal Employees (AFSCME) union executive for some time. More schools followed. These schools got noticed, often visited.

Andrekopolous backed the fearless teachers, who would say to anyone who asked that being entirely in charge of a school was a more daunting task than they knew. Hard work. But professionally fulfilling.

And each of the schools, all inside the circle of the district, had a memorandum of understanding (MOU) with the local National Education Association (NEA) chapter. These schools, numbering nearly a dozen then, were constantly buffeted by central office people who tried to enforce a single operating model on all schools (though as long as Andrekopolous was there, he supported them) and the local union chapter, which was (despite the MOUs they had signed) never comfortable with these schools operating outside the collective bargaining agreement.

So, the union people were always carping about them. And the central office would call a meeting for "principals" and then express wonderment over the dilemma these schools had.

One day Andrekopolous moved on. A new superintendent came. He had different ideas and did not like the schools that were run by teachers. He wanted all schools to be alike and big. Of all the schools that were teacher-led, only ALBA (Academia del Lenguaje y Bellas Artes) remains. Brenda Martinez, a lead teacher, says "that's because we're fighters." And it is because they consistently got good results in the midst of low expectations and always had a cadre of supportive parents. And Martinez says when she hears someone question the capacity of teachers to run a school, "it just makes my blood boil." And that is another reason why the school has survived successive superintendents who haven't liked the idea and a union always wary of this kind of change.

Some who read this account may wonder if the idea of teacher-powered schools in a district is a fantasy—something that seems like progress but is not likely to last. Sad as it is, it is just another lesson about the difficulty of changing what people think of as real school, especially in a district setting.

Joe Graba, already mentioned as a former legislator, was also a cofounder of EE and a former state higher education executive. He went to Milwaukee several times as a consultant. He remembers talking with a key member of the central office staff once, after making a presentation about the teacher-led schools. She was crestfallen, Graba recalls; "We just thought we were being fair (to treat all the schools alike)," she told him.

Boston

Sometimes schools, even in the most regulated environments in the United States, managed to be run mostly by teacher influence. The pilot schools in Boston are good examples. Dan French has long served the Center For Collaborative Education in Boston. He claims, with considerable justification, that having this nonprofit representing and watching the back of the Boston Pilot Schools is what made them endure, when others, like comparable schools in Milwaukee, largely withered and died.

Pilot schools in Boston were a teacher union reaction to the emergence of chartering, which became possible from a law passed in Massachusetts in 1993. By 1995, the pilot schools were launched, eventually growing to eighteen schools. When there is an opening for a new teacher, French said, "there are a ton of applications," though he admits that not every teacher in the Boston system aspires to work in one of these schools. "The hours tend to be longer, the work harder, but no veteran teacher," according to French, "ever wants to go back."

And the key officers of the Boston Teachers Union (BTU) agree. They even sponsored a school, known as the BTU school. With about 200 students, it is a teacher-powered school in Jamaica Plain serving kindergarten through eighth grade students. Betsy Drinan was the founder and is now the executive secretary-treasurer of the Boston Teachers Union. She pointed out that they got the "teacher-led option into the contract." A forty-year veteran of the district, Drinan does not require any prompting about the advantage of schools run by teachers. "There's just nothing like it," she says, "it's empowering, it's exciting."

Erik Berg, who is the vice president of the BTU, agrees. And when asked about whether teachers in charge of schools tend to put the needs and interests of students first, he says, "They have to. And even in a top-down curriculum situation, good teachers will find a way."

One of the nation's "ambassadors" for the teacher-powered movement, Taryn Snyder was in advertising for five years once she graduated from college, but, as she says, "I'd really rather be with kids." She's now also with the BTU school in Boston, and says, "she never looked back." But the kids come back, she adds, all the time, to the school they remember as they grow older.

New York City

New York City—isn't that the citadel of control? The absolute epitome of a larger-than-life district that always feels like only centralized control will let the people in charge know what is going on? This is another arena in which teachers can have extraordinary latitude, even though it is a traditional, rather than a teacher-powered, culture.

Spend an afternoon with the United Federation of Teachers (UFT) bunch on lower Broadway Avenue and listen to them talk; it is not the talk of those overcontrolled; it is the language of autonomy one hears. In a long afternoon, no one talked about typical union issues. It was all about the kids and about teachers having real influence over how kids learn. Jackie Bennett, who oversees the schools known as PROSE schools on behalf of the UFT, becomes super-animated when she talks about what happens in these schools, how they overcome odds, how they become memorable markers in young people's lives.

Nestled among the 1700 schools in New York city are about 170 PROSE schools; to get that designation you have to apply to the union and pass through a narrow needle's eye to qualify. Some schools are teacher-powered, but all get the opportunity to bend some of the rules of both the school district and the union; in return they offer innovations they will adopt. To become a PROSE school, approval is needed from a panel of evaluators that is 50 percent union-appointed, 25 percent from the city's Department of Education, and the rest from the Council of Administrative Supervisors. Sixty-five percent of faculty at that school have to agree, and if approved, the school has a five-year runway to show results.

One such school is the already-mentioned UAGC, carved out of the old Brandeis High School on Manhattan's Upper West Side. The Upper West Side is known as an affluent place. Green School (similar name but different from Denver's Green School), as most people call it, was not.

In 2013, the UAGC, populated from the lower baseline of New York City students, had a graduation rate of 39 percent; it was rated an "F" on the city's School Progress Report. Violence was an everyday occurrence.

That same year the city attracted a principal, Kerry Decker, who had done an impressive turnaround before elsewhere in the city. Her signature move, in addition to a battery of theories about how to build a culture of autonomy and voice—for both teachers and students—was what she called "shifting the power dynamic."

UAGC or the Green School is one of those places, despite being in an old building with three other schools, where a visitor feels the difference almost immediately. Students are busy, obviously motivated to do what they are doing. Teachers are animated, paying attention to what is going on. Allowing a measure of chaos amid the structure of school.

Within three years, Decker could say all those ugly numbers were getting better. The graduation rate went from 39 percent to 82 percent. Green became what the district called a "high impact" school. Even the special education students, who often took longer, were graduating at 72 percent, twenty-six points higher than the district average.

Any visitor would notice too that while most students were black or brown, most teachers were white. But teachers were candid about it. One young woman, originally from Wisconsin, said it took more than a year to build the kind of trust it takes to communicate, to be effective with these kids. But she does not aspire to leave now.

And even though the school has a principal, the teachers feel like they call the shots. And that is what makes the school what it is.

South Dakota

Sometimes a whole state, even with smaller populations, can try to get teachers more at the forefront of decisions. Julie Matheison is in charge of getting schools committed to personalized learning in South Dakota. She has nineteen schools participating, a lot for South Dakota, twelve of which have more than the average percentage of students qualifying for free or reduced price lunches, a proxy for poverty. It adds up to some 5000 students. She is pushing what she calls "learner agency" and reports that it is catching on. This is one step short of giving teachers full control over what matters.

But the legacy system is sticky. The idea of what real school is, the dominant mindset, dies hard. As Matheison puts it, "If we say first, second, and fourth graders will be in the same area, people just lose their minds. We surveyed communities and parents are telling us things like they want the things associated with personalization, but they are alarmed by change."

A NEW DEAL

And that is exactly what policymakers face. That is what compels a new deal.

Students actually get the change in the model right away, though. Walter Cortina, who has been homeless and knows poverty intimately, is now a student at High School for the Recording Arts (HSRA) in St. Paul. When he looked at the principles for teacher-schools, he smiled right away and said, "Yes. That's what I've been looking for" (and what HSRA now provides for him).

Cortina, liking the outdoors, would love Wildlands School in Wisconsin. One of its founders, Paul Tweed, says it is simpler than most people realize that it is a matter of "getting to know the kids." His founding partner, Liz Seubert, still young but hooked entirely on being in charge of the school, points to the students too and says, "That's the real power."

Wildlands gets its power from being different, from making students "part of the team." It is a public school authorized by the Augusta school district in central Wisconsin, not far from the college town of Eau Claire. It is locally governed and teacher-managed. It is not traditional in any way. Supplies are more likely to be clothes suitable for curiosity jaunts around the school lands, along with copious quantities of bug spray and the obligatory GPS units.

Wildlands gets noticed, not because teachers have such prominent influence but because it gets results. Because students like the way they are learning.

Ingersoll, as a professor, sees all this from his university perch. He stands out among the academic voices for teachers getting more control over their work. As already mentioned, Ingersoll is aghast at the attitudes of people as he travels around the United States making presentations: "People just cannot imagine teachers being in charge of a school."

Ingersoll's fix: start smaller. Adopt the narrative of enlarging the teacher's role. Let it grow. That is the way successful industries practice innovation.

Early in this chapter, the century-long deal the public had with teachers was described. And the effort to change the deal unilaterally in order to lean on teachers for more accountability was added starting in 2001.

It is time now for a new deal—one that offers authority and demands accountability. A deal that says to any group of willing teachers who say they will take responsibility for a new or an existing school—if they are in charge—go ahead. The public will give you full authority and real autonomy in that school. You, in turn, give the public what it is looking for: full accountability for results. That is a deal that neither the public nor the teachers should turn down.

Chapter 3

Trust the Teachers—Finally
The Movement Itself

Trusting Teachers with School Success, the 2013 book written by Kim Farris-Berg and Ed Dirkswager with Amy Junge, boosted what was an inchoate initiative to something looking more like a real movement—increasingly growing around the country.

And though their research was mostly through surveys and field visits, they found remarkable parallels between schools we did not yet call teacher-powered and high-performing organizations in other industries.

Farris-Berg and Dirkswager listed, in education terms, what high-performing organizations do, which most schools do not, and what they would try to learn about schools selected to study. Did those schools:

- Accept ownership: Welcome authority and responsibility for making decisions and be accountable for outcomes?
- Innovate: Take risks to try creative new things, challenge old processes and continuously adapt?
- Share purpose: Seek clarity and buy-in to the mission, values, goals, and standards of practice?
- Collaborate: Establish a culture of interdependence characterized by an open flow of ideas, listening to and understanding others, and valuing differences?
- Lead effectively: Expect leadership from all and perceive leadership as in service to all?
- Function as learners: Establish a culture characterized by a sense of common challenge and discovery, rather than a culture that imparts information?
- Avoid insularity: Learn from and be sensitive to the external environment?
- Motivate: Be engaged, motivated, and motivating?
- Assess performance: Set and measure progress toward goals and act upon results to improve performance?

Unlike some other researchers, they ruled out using test scores as the measure, believing that achievement was more than statistics. They quoted William Ouchi in his assertion that it is "the approach to managing the schools" that matters, and that school leaders should have "the freedom to be entrepreneurs."

They had encountered the early work of Ingersoll at the University of Pennsylvania, who had concluded that workers were not the problem with the American education system. They noticed that he had said in an article, "It makes no sense to hold people accountable for something they do not control or to give people control over something for which they are not held accountable."

Calling teacher autonomy a "promising strategy," Farris-Berg and Dirkswager made a serious contribution to starting the modern movement of teachers calling the shots in schools.

Now it is 2020. There is a movement and it is growing. But it remains small. And most people, according to survey research done in 2013, do not know that teachers could have real professional autonomy, that they could call the shots in school.

WHERE DID THIS TEACHER-POWERED MOVEMENT COME FROM?

Although the exact history of the first schools to be entirely under the control of teachers is a bit fuzzy, probably the first such schools in the United States, dating back to the 1970s, were the San Francisco Community School and the High School in the Community in New Haven, Connecticut. Neither one is still teacher-powered, but they were apparently the first.

And Kolderie recalls the issue of teachers forming partnerships or becoming owners of schools was being discussed as early as 1982 in many national and regional meetings. The idea was pushed by Ruth Ann Olson in Minneapolis. She actually showed how groups of teachers, organized into private practice, could be hired to do work for schools.

Practically, though, the movement began in the 1990s with schools like Minnesota New Country School (MNCS), first in Le Sueur and then permanently in Henderson, Minnesota, and in its earliest form a school within a public school district. It is now a chartered school, the teachers operating under Minnesota cooperatives law.

The photo (Figure 3.1) of MNCS students looks like the marketing department of a start-up firm. And the photo itself, as the computers in the picture reveal, is about twenty years old. This heavily visited school always strikes a stranger as not looking like "school." Looking carefully, one finds the adults.

Figure 3.1 Students at Work. *Ted Kolderie Photograph.*

They are advisors as much as teachers, planning guides, still in charge but not making a big deal about it.

The school has always had a substantial number of students classified as special education students, including some with autism. But most visitors cannot tell which students they are. They are, as much as is possible, fully assimilated into the school's way of doing things. They are doing projects like the other students. This population tends to grow because of the school's reputation for helping kids with any kind of disability prosper.

Even in Minnesota, and despite its long history of success and its higher-than-average retention rates of faculty, the school is regarded as a problem by some in the state education bureaucracy. They have had difficulty getting licenses, for example, for the kind of teachers they need. The school does not fit the mold of what people think of as real school.

The point is that the movement of teacher-powered schools, while still in its early stages, is not new. It has roots at least a quarter century old. But it is growing mostly like groundcover. Staring at it, even for a long time, and little growth is discernible. But if the look is every six months or so, there is growth.

Many schools have changed, adapting to changed realities in the world and in their quest for what works best for their students. But teacher-powered schools have a look about them; it is one not easy to describe but necessarily there.

Maybe that "look" is about student motivation, or even student "agency" as it is now called so often. An observer senses that students are actually doing something. They are not sitting in orderly rows passively taking in knowledge. They are actively in pursuit of something, nearly all the time.

TIMELINE OF TEACHER-POWERED SCHOOLS

In an initial phase of managing a national network, Education Evolving and the Center for Teacher Quality collaborated on the challenge. Here is a timeline of major developments affecting the movement, which EE now manages nationally.

- 2002: *Teachers as Owners*—2002: This book, edited by Ed Dirkswager, focused on teacher partnerships.
- 2003: Public Agenda Foundation publishes in the Phi Delta Kappan a survey in which the question is asked about teachers' willingness to work in a school run by teachers, and the question says "a charter school." Even with this skewing of the question, an aggregate 58 percent of respondents were affirmative. Nearly two-thirds of newer teachers and half the veterans agreed.
- 2013: *Trusting Teachers with School Success—What Happens When Teachers Call the Sho*ts by Kim Farris-Berg and Ed Dirkswager with Amy Junge. This book extended the premise embraced in *Teachers as Owners*. From the research behind this book came the first ten autonomies and the eight teacher practices; and it showed the wide variety of schools already working. There would be no national network or initiative or the eventual movement without this book's impact.
- 2014: Launch of the Teacher Powered Initiative as a joint project of Education Evolving and the Center for Teacher Quality (CTQ) in 2014. A big year for what would become a movement, it was the year a white paper was posted on a new website and the term *teacher-powered* was adopted to describe this growing group of schools. Later that year Kim Farris-Berg (of EE) and Lori Nazareno (of CTQ) produced the first *Steps Guide to Creating a Teacher-Powered School.*
- 2014: Widmeyer Communications (now a division of the Finn Group), with offices in Washington D.C. and New York city, published the results of their national survey and teachers and parents. The survey results found 78 percent of teachers saying that teacher professional partnerships were a good

idea. Over half of teachers said they were interested in working in such a school. And parents were even more supportive.
- 2015: The first cohort of teacher-powered ambassadors was named to represent the new movement around the country. The first national conference was held in Minneapolis, Minnesota.
- 2017: The second national conference was held in Los Angeles, California.
- 2018: Regional networks were formed for Minnesota, Wisconsin, Massachusetts, and the Los Angeles areas. The third national conference was held in Boston, Massachusetts.

As of the winter of 2020 there are now some 150 schools that have been identified in twenty states of the United States. According to Amy Junge and Alex Vitrella of Education Evolving, it is a constantly if slow-growing movement, with lots of variation. "If you've seen one teacher-powered school, you've seen just one school," they both say. The schools identified have consideration variation, but the common bond is a reverence for teacher influence over what matters for school and student success.

Since there are so many variations, EE uses a set of fifteen autonomies to perform a qualifying look at a potential school, all subject to constraints embodied in state or federal laws or regulations listed in Table 3.1. A school must demonstrate it has all or some of at least four of these to qualify for listing; the average of schools they have classified though is more than ten. Most autonomies can be full or partial, depending on the structural circumstances of each school.

SURVEYING TEACHERS AND PARENTS

There is little if any remaining uncertainty about whether the idea is popular. Teacher-powered schools pass every known test, especially the most important one, attracting talent from the ranks of existing teachers.

In the annual poll (2019) conducted by the *Phi Delta Kappan* (PDK), half the teachers once again said they had "seriously considered" leaving the profession. And just short of half of those surveyed said the communities they served did not value them. Fifty-two percent said they would strike over school standards and 42 percent over teaching conditions. Perhaps most of the teachers do not know what those conditions might be.

As the timeline entries show, another set of results dates back to 2003 from Public Agenda in the Phi Delta Kappa poll: this poll showed 58 percent of teachers willing to work in a chartered school, if it were run by teachers. Biasing the question to make it necessary to agree to chartering did not appear to lower the enthusiasm for the teacher powered model. Two thirds of

Table 3.1 Teacher-Powered School Autonomies

Autonomy	Description
Learning program	Philosophy of learning, materials and methods, curriculum and learning environment, including use of technology
School policy	Decisions that affect the daily operation of the school, including homework, disciplinary methods, and whom to hire to assist teachers
Schedule	The school calendar, including daily start and end times, and how student and teacher time is used.
Teacher work hours	How many hours a day teachers work, an autonomy especially sensitive in unionized environments, where there may be Memoranda of Understanding or Elect to Work agreements to formalize the deviation from the usual arrangement.
Selecting colleagues	Decisions about who is selected as a teacher or staff for the school. These determinations often involve parents and community members. Some teams may select but not dismiss, an example of partial autonomy.
Choosing school leaders	Principals, lead teachers, and key committees.
Professional development	How resources are allocated as well as the focus of the effort.
Evaluation	Methods used for choosing people, committees, or a peer-based evaluation system.
Tenure	Terms of tenure and how the process is implemented.
Terminating or transferring colleagues	Dismissing or recommending dismissal of teachers or classified staff, who in some cases go into a district pool but leave the school.
Budget	How all resources are used and what priorities will govern choices.
Compensation for staff	Control over the salary formulas and processes, determining how to compensate teachers and school leaders.
Staffing pattern	Determining how to use personnel, including substituting paraprofessionals, for teachers and making some positions less than full time.
Assessment	Freedom for teachers to decide whether to take, when to take, and how to count assessments from districts, charter management organizations, or charter authorizers. State mandated assessment are excepted.
Other assessment	Provision for multiple measures of student success, such as student engagement or ability to defend a portfolio of work, as negotiated with the district, charter management organization, or charter authorizer.

Source: Teacher-Powered Schools.

teachers with more than twenty years of service said "yes," along with more than half of those with less than twenty years.

Then, in 2013, Scott Widmeyer, CEO of Widmeyer Communications, had a team conduct a national survey of teachers and parents to see what they thought about teachers being in charge of what matters in school. Figure 3.2 shows the results.

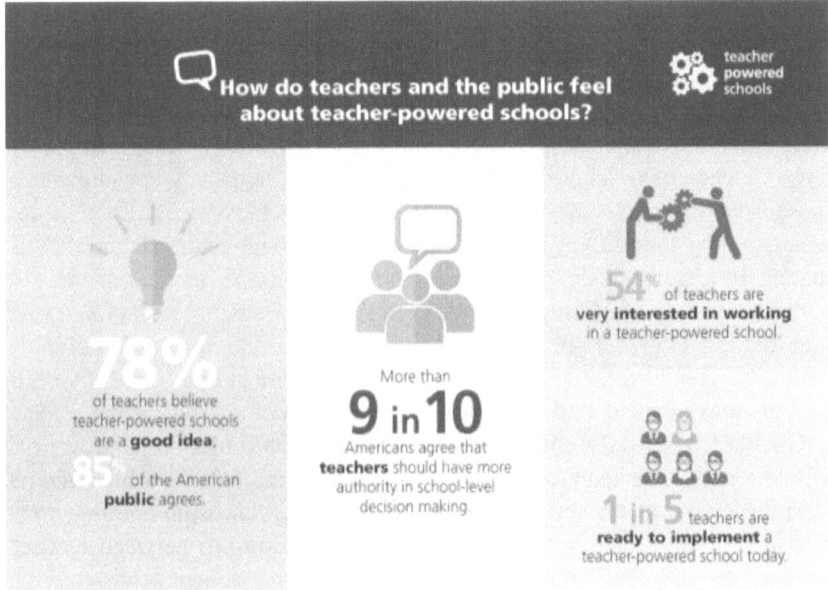

Figure 3.2 **Authority Mismatch.** *Teacher-Powered Schools.*

The results distributed widely in 2014 were stunning. Seventy-eight percent of teachers agreed that the teacher-powered idea was a good one. And that already high percentage was exceeded by the enthusiasm of parents for the idea; 85 percent of them agreed. And more than nine out of ten respondents thought that giving teachers more authority over decision-making in schools was a good thing.

Of special note was the percentage of teachers interested in working in such a school, if they had an opportunity; 54 percent of them said yes. And one in every five were ready to sign up right away.

STUDENT ACHIEVEMENT

Anyone who has tried to dig up philanthropic support for the teacher-powered movement can testify to the number-one question that program officers in the education sector have: Do the students do better in these schools? Naturally, they do not want to spend money on losing propositions. For a time, there was only anecdotal evidence about student achievement.. And only survey data that showed students were satisfied being in these schools, more motivated.

A deeper dive shows a mountain of previous academic interest in "collective teacher efficacy," which when translated into terms ordinary people use, sounds a lot like teacher-powered schools. Roger Goddard, for example, who is a professor at the University of Michigan's School of Education produced considerable research on the correlation between teachers having collaborative influence over school improvement and what happens when students at those schools take state-mandated tests about achievement. Even if test results are by themselves limited indicators of student achievement, they do matter. In a study Goddard put online in 2004, with Yvonne Goddard, also at the University of Michigan, he showed the achievement results for several hundred fourth graders in math and reading in one large urban district in the Midwest. The correlations were there and they were strong. Collective efficacy by teachers and student achievement went up or down together.

Goddard previously collaborated with Wayne Hoy and Anita Hoy in an article for the *American Education Research Journal* in 2000, which laid out both the model of collective efficacy and the effects of using an operational measure to confirm that there was in fact a relationship between teachers have a "shared belief" in their collective efficacy and student achievement in reading and mathematics.

And, in a subsequent inquiry, published online in 2017, with Linda Skria and Serena Solloum, Goddard took on the equity issue. In a large urban district in Texas, from which he sampled several hundred elementary and middle school students, he found that having a principal who believed in and practiced serious teacher collaboration on issues affecting school improvement reduced the "academic disadvantage" by half.

In 2011 Rachel J. Eels, the dean of the College of Arts and Sciences at Concordia University in Chicago, as a part of her doctoral program at Loyola University in Chicago, conducted a meta-analysis of twenty-six studies, finding also that teachers in a collective form, collaborating, had a strongly positive effect on student achievement.

Note that the schools in these studies are not teacher-powered schools. Some of the studies were done when the teacher-powered idea was embryonic. Eels wraps her work in the framework of "social cognition theory," but in her writing, she apparently cannot resist a comment about the system. "The current antagonism between schools and teachers has the potential to corrode any sense of collective efficacy that has been built in our schools," she writes.

About the same time, John Shindler, who is a professor at California State University in Los Angeles, published his book *Transformative Classroom Management*. In his book, he described the natural state of school as a harmonious, productive, satisfying place. In contrast, many teachers see the classrooms they work in as full of hostility, apathy, and outright resistance, Shindler says.

Shindler explains the approaches that emphasize a love of learning, better engagement of students, creating a culture of respect and listening. He advocates building an actual social contract for the school experience. His work about school "climate" has become quite influential.

What these researchers describe is what teachers do, in effect, when they are in control of what matters in a school. That is what the teacher-powered idea is all about.

More recently, a doctoral student finishing her degree at the University of Minnesota, Sara Kemper, stumbled on to the teacher-powered movement by showing up at a national conference. As she put it, "Now I had my idea for a research project." She focused for her dissertation on the effects of teachers having real collective authority in their schools. Her sample was three schools—all teacher-powered, but having widely different ranges of autonomy and other differences, a situation common in the movement. She selected one school on the east coast, one on the west coast and one in middle America. Figure 3.3 shows the differences she found in teacher satisfaction.

Kemper also surveyed some 350 teachers in 40 different teacher-powered schools to enhance her data. As expected, she found the higher levels of commitment and satisfaction anyone would expect of teachers these days.

Then, there is Ingersoll, who in 2017 completed a major study the results of which were published, among other places, in the *American Educator* magazine of the American Federation of Teachers. Ingersoll, a professor of sociology and education at the University of Pennsylvania, is the same academic who said a decade earlier that whoever controlled teachers' work, it certainly was not teachers, assembled the most robust database he had ever had and drew conclusions about student achievement in schools where teachers had "more influence."

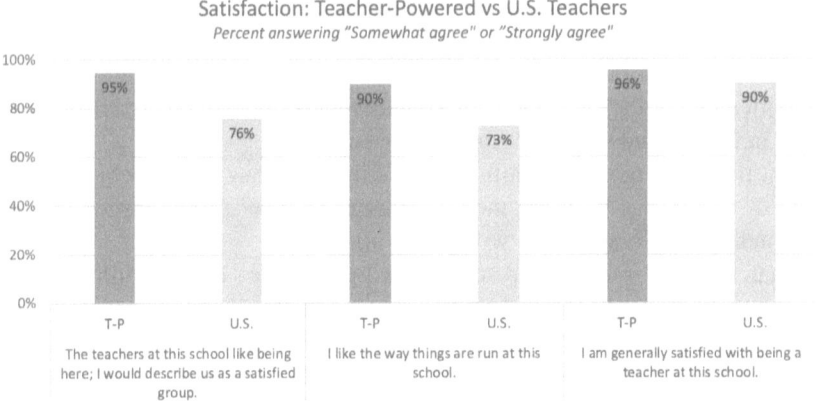

Figure 3.3 **Satisfaction Comparisons.** *Sara Kemper Research.*

This database comprised responses from 900,000 teachers in 25,000 schools scattered over twelve states in the period from 2011 to 2015. Those data clearly supported the theory that suggests where teachers have real influence over what matters, the results for students are better.

After listing the predictable areas in which teachers might aspire to have more influence in schools, Ingersoll found that teachers had little influence (an average of 6 percent) on budget matters and a lot in some areas, as high as 88 percent) on teaching matters. Curiously, they had only "middling" influence over disciplinary matters or overall school planning—both areas in which their influence was highly correlated with student success.

So, Ingersoll now says, without any hesitation, that schools where teachers had more influence, students do better. Simple as that. Maybe not surprising, but a major finding.

That finding should surprise everyone who thinks top down, who believes that no school can succeed without a charismatic principal, without someone telling the others what to do.

Ingersoll used state tests, admitting that these were the only available metric he could find. And knowing how they varied from state to state, he made his comparisons all within states, comparing schools on that test to other schools in the state. He found anywhere from 10 to 20 percentage points difference from teacher influence.

No one should dismiss the finding, he said. "The more voice teachers have the better students do. That is, in my field, a strong finding, certainly statistically significant."

TEACHER RETENTION

As already mentioned but this time because it makes teachers stay in the career, researchers have looked at retention. Across many interviews, and at every national gathering, anyone will find teachers in these schools telling how much work they do, how they sometimes feel burned out; most say they have never worked so hard in their entire careers.

But then they nearly all shift to stories that illustrate how teaching in this kind of school has been the most fulfilling experience they have ever had. And nearly no one says they will give it up.

That is called retention. And comparing the rates of retention between teacher-powered schools and other schools tells the whole story: Data are spotty on this variable, but anecdotally, it sure seems like it is much higher than the industry average. Certainly, it varies school by school, and the ratio is an extrapolation from sampling, but the bottom line, as Kemper observed, is greater satisfaction.

Retention in the education industry is the system that tracks whether teachers stay on the job or leave for another school or just leave the career entirely. In a presentation in Saint Paul late fall of 2019, Ingersoll would say that "the conventional wisdom is that we have teacher shortages. True enough. But it is only in fields like science or math or special education." But then, he tells people, notice how often we see a spate of public service messages—all designed to lure more into the field, and most often not to specific fields or levels of schooling. "The public is treated to cries about shortages, about the need for more teachers to join the field."

Instead, Ingersoll went on, the nation ought to focus on *why* teachers leave. "It's a retention problem, not one of recruitment," he said. The implication: it is not a very good job for many teachers; and certainly not something young people with choices to make want to do, once they discover what the job is actually like.

Academics like raw numbers, so here are some, Ingersoll continued, illustrating that teaching in too many schools has become a "professional revolving door." Of the 3,385,171 teachers today, 531,340 will leave every year—either for another school (likely lower poverty or less urban) or leave altogether. So, the industry recruits an average of 343,955 new teachers each year.

The onset of the pandemic and its roiling effect on schools has apparently caused many teachers to consider giving it all up. In a late spring 2020 survey by *Education Week*'s Research Center, some 44 percent of today's teachers report they are considering leaving their classrooms, at least by next fall.

Private industry long ago discovered the costs of turnover. Education has not as yet, according to Ingersoll. "Costs are huge," he said. "That's why we have the shortages we do and, in addition to the time and money costs, student achievement and overall school cohesion are casualties," he said. And turnover is right up there with child care workers, paralegals, and correctional workers; it is twice that of nurses.

If retention is a crisis, how severe is it? Ingersoll said that the leave rate was an annual average of 44.6 percent across all the schools he surveyed (and that is exclusive of the effects of the pandemic). After about five years, the rate levels off. The question becomes: Why. Table 3.2 below shows what teachers reported as reasons.

The reason most often cited was "dissatisfaction," which raises the next question: Dissatisfaction with what? Table 3.3 is based on data from public districts only, but shows what teachers said was dissatisfying.

If you have a leaky bucket, and the education industry certainly does, Ingersoll maintained, any school or district could give teachers more voice, more influence over decisions that affect the school. It correlates highly, he said. "It is a major finding and school people should pay attention."

Table 3.2 General Reasons for Quitting

Retirement	18.7
School staffing actions	20.2
Family and personal reasons	44.4
To another job, possible in education	36.0
Dissatisfaction	56.7

Source: Richard Ingersoll, professor, University of Pennsylvania.

Table 3.3 Reasons for Leaving

Percent of teachers citing reason	Reason
60.6	Accountability and testing practices
57.8	Administrations
51.6	Lack of autonomy and influence
50.1	Classroom intrusions
48.2	Student disciplinary situations
47.2	Poor facilities and inadequate resources
40.6	Dissatisfaction with teaching assignment
29.5	Class size too large

Source: Richard Ingersoll, professor, University of Pennsylvania.

Ingersoll went on to point out the steadily growing movement of teachers being in charge of schools. Most schools out there are making little or no use of this teacher potential, he said.

IT IS THE SYSTEM

There is really no way to avoid it: unless the system is changed, there is no hope of much improvement in student outcomes. And it will not be easy. Most adults, even that majority that is earnest about the mission, will resist change. It is a natural reflexive reaction. So, change must come from the outside. Perhaps you have to be "outside" to see the necessity for change.

In *Disrupting Class*, the underlying implication of the book was that change would come from technology. Technology is making a difference but not at the speed the authors anticipated. State lawmakers are the key. They are the architects of education policy design in their states. Education is in state constitutions; nowhere does it appear in national founding documents. Legislators can, if they will, change the system. The system itself is slow, preferring in too many places to do what may have once worked but now seems obsolete and out of place to many students.

EE's Amy Junge was keynoting the Coalition of Independent Charter Schools national conference in Albuquerque in the fall of 2019. She reminisced about growing up, wanting to be a teacher. "You played school with stuffed animals," she told the audience, "or maybe you were lucky and had one of those life-changing teachers . . ."

She told them that all teachers need "connections, support, respect and value—a collaborative culture." That is what the teacher-powered movement celebrates, she said. We move "decisions closer to the educators who work with the students every day."

The system, or the education industry, claims the same thing. But it does not often deliver. Junge continued, "The traditional system was not designed to meet the needs of *all* students. It wasn't designed for equity—either for students or teachers."

That is the core problem. The dominant system was never designed to help every student realize full potential. It was a sorting procedure, a compliance machine, and too often it still is.

When Susan Moore Johnson, now a research professor at the Harvard Graduate School of Education, reported for *Education Week* on the evaluation of the Bill and Melinda Gates Foundation's $575 million attempt to raise student performance levels of low-income and minorities by having better teachers, she described how the project retained the best teachers and dismissed the poor ones.

After sorting through test scores, graduation rates, and the results of the National Assessment of Education Progress (NAEP), evaluators found no appreciable gains in student performance. What they did find was a significant difference if the school itself had structures that supported learning. If the schools authorized teachers to select the new teachers. If the teachers were the leaders in the school. That is exactly what distinguishes the teacher-powered schools movement.

But the model gains acceptance slowly. Maybe Tom Toch's explanation is correct: "After 60 years of collective bargaining and almost a century of every school having a principal, you'd have to expect that 'teacher-powered' threatens that model." Toch has had many roles in the industry; he has seen it all and now heads FutureEd at Georgetown University.

Yet individual schools show how different it can be. Talking with Josef Donnelly, a teacher at the teacher-powered International Community School in New York City, he cheerfully admits he is not a veteran. And the school in which he teaches is populated by immigrants, none of whom have been in the United States for more than four years. He is young. But he has already figured out that it is collaboration among professionals that pays off, that makes some schools different from the dominant system.

But the issue is not whether schools have principals. The issue is how much authority teachers have over what matters. The teacher-powered movement offers Figure 3.4 as evidence of what teachers think.

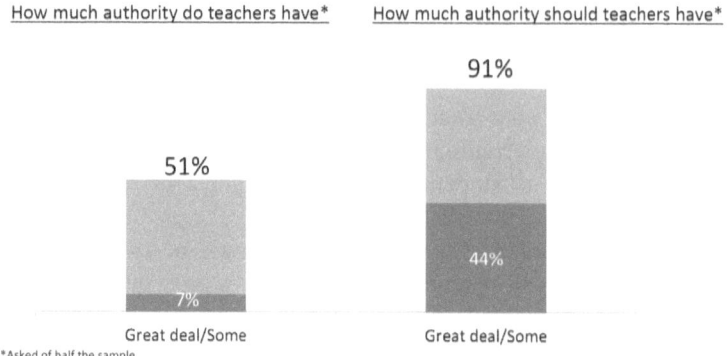

Figure 3.4 **Facts about Teacher-Powered Schools.** *Teacher-Powered Schools.*

Donnelly's school has a principal, but, as he says, she mostly "defends and deflects." They know they are working in a complex system that prizes compliance. They have learned what they can do. And teachers there know, as Donnelly puts it, that "It's real when they can control their work—the curriculum and all that matters for success."

Donnelly's school succeeds well beyond the odds of its student population. Teachers like him would not stay, he says, if the school was not a place where students could succeed.

THE BURNING QUESTION

Anyone not immersed in the industry can see, almost immediately, that the system succeeds in resisting fundamental change. That will not change. Even a sometimes advocate of teachers being in charge says, as does Jeff Park, an officer working in the Aurora, Colorado, schools, "I don't know of any NFL team that doesn't have a coach." The notion that some singular person, which usually carries the title of principal, has to be in charge of what matters for student and school success.

And sometimes, audacity, a bold move to get attention, to foster change, does not seem to pay off, especially in a system so resistant to change. Kolderie and Graba took two teachers from teacher-powered schools—one from Saint Paul and another from Milwaukee—to see the secretary of Education, Arne Duncan, in April of 2010. Carrie Bakken was a lead teacher of Avalon in Saint Paul, a charter school. Brenda Martinez was a lead teacher for ALBA school in Milwaukee. Both are still in place.

Bakken and Martinez described what is different about those schools. How it affects students—with their lives, their aspirations for the future. They talked about teachers, about their extraordinary retention rates, about good academic results with students who have sometimes been written off by the system.

Duncan assembled his entire senior staff to listen and ask questions, so he must have thought this was a significant development to take note of. He asked Bakken why there were not more such schools, since they made such obvious common sense? The answer would be obvious too. Because as time passed, and it was clear that Duncan would not do anything to advance the teacher-powered movement, the audacity did not seem to pay dividends. Such is the tenacity of the idea of real school.

Avalon School in Saint Paul is by itself a major story. It opened back in 2001 and is now housed in a remodeled building on the western edge of Saint Paul. Still led by Bakken and the team of teachers there, it is the most complete teacher-powered model in the country. The teachers are organized to make all the decisions. They do hire a few people to do key work, like preparing the budget. And they give released time to lead teachers for administrative work. They have committees for everything and after a few years of talking too much and deciding too little, they got very efficient. They use an old Quaker method of showing fingers of support for whatever might be on the table. Five is right on. Four means, "I do have a question." Three may signify struggling support. Four is a warning sign and a fist means No Way.

Widmeyer, who had done the national survey for EE, was a guest at one of Avalon's weekly "management" meetings where the teachers gather to share notes and get decisions. The meeting is organized and takes only an hour before school starts. Asked afterward what his takeaways were, he said, "It was the most efficient meeting I ever saw, but (and here he paused a few seconds) I could never figure out who was in charge." What he saw was intentional. Sure, there was an agenda and responsibility for explanations went around the room. Everyone knew who the lead teachers were, but in that setting, it really didn't matter. And it didn't show.

And if you observe the students, talking in hallways, sitting on the floor, conferring with advisors (teachers), you might conclude that not much was going on, no real schooling. But just interview any student, and quickly it is clear that much is happening. It just does not look like real school—the way most people still think of it.

Kids are working on projects or thinking about their next one. They studying something, like math, which often happens in groups. Informal settings seem to trump formal ones.

Mindsets, though, are hard to change. And the experience with Secretary Duncan reinforces the notion of building the movement from the ground up, not the top down.

Yet, despite moments of discouragement, the movement of teacher-powered schools, continues to grow. And the enthusiasm for the model is growing along with the number of schools. But not very rapidly. Not fast enough to be noticed by major media. Not significant enough, by the numbers, to look like a solution to what ails the system.

The body of research is growing that answers the question long posed by critics and funders. Kids do better where teachers have more influence. So if the kids do better, and professional retention is higher, why does not the movement grow faster? What does not growth like groundcover become something more like wildfire? But should it grow faster? Those are the questions for the next chapter.

Chapter 4

Hit the Accelerator
How the Movement Could Grow

What is the number one reason why the movement of teacher-powered schools is growing slowly? The answer (again) may be too obvious: not enough teachers know it is an option.

And this is exactly what Widmeyer found when his east coast firm was commissioned to do the most comprehensive survey of teachers done in modern times. "Most teachers had to be told about the movement," he recalled back in 2014.

Here is what making the movement bigger, faster would require:

- Massive publicity aimed at teachers
- Documentation of the movement
- More research—particularly about student achievement
- Cadres of support—region by region
- Grants—legislative and philanthropic
- Retirement and benefit programs
- Teacher preparation for a different role

CONDUCT MASSIVE PUBLICITY

The first priority would be to conduct a major publicity campaign aimed at all the teachers who might agree to work in a teacher-powered school. In the early years of EE's partnership with CTQ following the Widmeyer survey, the organizations pursued major publicity for the idea. The staff at both EE and CTQ knew that in a profession where nearly half the new entrants give up the job, and possibly the career, in the first five years, letting them know that the job might be something other than what they know today might make the critical difference.

But today's environment is noisy. It is not easy breaking through, getting attention, even for the best ideas. It will take some resources to ensure that teachers know that working in a school that is led by teachers is a professional option.

Why are many teachers not aware this is possible? Are those young people on picket lines in recent years saying they want more pay, lower class sizes, or are they saying "Either this job gets better or I'm out of here." No one knows for sure, but some union leaders have thoughts.

John Wright, an officer of the National Education Association in charge of strategy (and the former president of the Arizona Teachers Union), posed in 2019 a haunting question. He said there are at least two small education movements in the United States. One gets a lot of press, referring to eruptions from teachers in states like West Virginia, Oklahoma, and Arizona.

While there have been protests or strikes in Oakland, Denver, and Chicago as recently as 2019, Wright says people should pay attention to teacher walkouts in states where the legal structure is hostile to bargaining, to unions themselves. In West Virginia, lawmakers almost immediately issued threats of firing, or fining, or introducing bills to authorize vouchers or charters.

Wright observes though that leading this charge were those younger teachers, just the kind who, if the job does not get better, will walk away from teaching altogether. "Even though we are maybe the largest union in the world," he says, "we could not have orchestrated this. It just happened. And we are learning from it."

But then he posed the critical question: "What if those teachers discover the other small movement in the country, what if they find out they could be fully in charge of what matters in a school. What might they do then?" No one really knows, but it is the right question. And why wouldn't the public have an interest in teachers—the best ones coming on the scene—knowing that they could call the shots themselves?

Massive publicity would be expensive, even if some of the effort was donated. There are thousands of private sector companies with giving programs, not to mention private and community foundations and a multitude of individual donors to good causes. But a budget for publicity would still be a necessity.

Then there is social media. Just imagine the viral tendencies let loose among teachers across the country! Once the movement starts moving around on social media, gets picked up on the latest feed and teachers (and school board members) start looking at Facebook pages (even if mostly older people do that these days) devoted to these schools, perhaps the scene will shift. And toward faster growth.

What people think of as social media changes rapidly. Today it is Instagram and TikTok that young people are talking about. What some of us thought was market-dominant becomes yesterday's news fast. Obviously, someone has to be experienced and shrewd enough to orchestrate all this activity and that may require resources, but it is possible to do. Again, EE and CTQ started the publicity push. And EE continues to do it at the scale they can afford. More resources might accelerate the effects.

Parents are another key constituency. Their interests in alternatives certainly drove the chartered school movement to faster growth, so much so that such schools are now in the crosshairs of controversy. When there were only a few, it did not seem to matter much. The publicity campaign should focus on key intermediary organizations whose word commands the respect of parents looking for the best educational experiences for their kids.

Those who would limit choice for parents often imply that low-income parents care less about what is happening with their kids. That is just wrong. In many urban settings, parents, even and especially low-income and minority parents, have become the main disruptors of the system. They demand and get better experiences for their kids.

Remember those Milwaukee schools? When asked about the role of parents, teachers did not say they were the problem, or people just to be tolerated or talked to once or twice a year. One teacher volunteered that more than a hundred parents showed up most days—just to help out. The teachers running the school regarded them as partners, people essential to the success of the students.

Finally, there are unions. No organization can mobilize the army of teachers as fast or as well as the unions do. If they ever sign on to support the teacher-powered movement, they can and will make a major difference. The landscape of what is possible would then shift toward managing growth, not having to cause it.

Most observers are skeptical about unions ever supporting this movement. They have good reasons. But most observers also concede that unions have to change, along with nearly every other institution. Trying to stay the same and succeed at it is a loser's game. And there are in fact conversations—sometimes serious arguments—going on within unions at the local, state, and national levels. Arguments about what kind of future they want. Arguments about the wisdom of repositioning what the union stands for, who it supports and why. Unions are, in most respects, democracies; they do what most of their members want done. Once demand shifts enough, they will change.

Demand is the driver of change in this whole society. So, raising the demand among every key constituency is the path toward more effective publicity. And given the imperative of finding a better idea, the demand should be growing.

DOCUMENT THE MOVEMENT

Lists matter. Longer lists matter more. Big lists compel interest. They grab attention.

There are likely more teacher-powered schools than those known to the national network organizers. Today the organizers list 150 schools across twenty states. Using their fifteen autonomies to evaluate which schools qualify, they do diligent research about each one that applies or they hear about. But that takes time—an average of eight person-hours per school, according to Junge.

Just imagine for a moment that there were thousands (rather than hundreds) of teacher-powered schools. Imagine the buzz, the impact, the effects on what it means to be a teacher, the reshaping of a whole profession.

Like it or not, the United States has a culture where numbers matter. Bigger numbers get more attention. And once this movement gets serious attention and reaches whatever the tipping point is, it is almost bound to grow, and a lot faster.

What is now needed are the resources to accelerate the documentation of schools that are already teacher-powered but not counted in the movement's totals. Big grants from national foundations would be helpful, but even more helpful would be a pattern of smaller grants from regional and local philanthropies—organizations interested in getting one of America's largest systems to change, to serve all the kids, not just those who are ready. The teacher-powered movement may prove to be bigger than the national network managers at present know.

ANSWER THE OBVIOUS QUESTIONS

As mentioned in the section about student achievement, if anyone contacted a program officer of a foundation where a match of interests looked good, the question almost predictably came, usually early in the conversation: Do the kids in teacher-powered schools do better? What they meant of course was do they score better on the end of year standardized tests?

For many years, there was no good answer to that question. Now there is. And many academic researchers are tuning into the key questions. And they are looking for funding to do that research. Some are even broadening the definition of achievement, a welcome change.

Ingersoll, whose work has already been cited, also suggests that researchers do a new look at other aspects of "teacher voice." You can control factors like poverty, urban or suburban, etc. If you have a school with high turnover, that is going to affect scores. You would guess there is a negative impact. In the work he is already done he says,

> I just used a couple sets. But there are many other things we asked teachers. There's data in there that I haven't analyzed yet. So, I've got a whole wish list. So we showed that significantly better achievement—but how does it differentiate large and small schools, urban or suburban? So the next step is to disaggregate. We found positive effects but how "robust" are they? Do they show up in high poverty schools, for example? We did a lot of aggregating. So we need to do disaggregation seriously. With quantitative analysis. We spent a lot of background time trying to be sure that we'd have a quality database.

The percentage of young people who do not finish even high school is astonishing.

Districts brag if their rates of graduation—itself a volatile measure—are in the high numbers. But what about those who quit? Or those who are encouraged to quit, as in suspended from school. Why does this happen? If some student behavior was the stated reason, what is behind that behavior? Why do bright young people reject school, even when they are told that doing well there makes a big difference for the rest of their lives? Why does society, year after year, tolerate the waste of so many young lives? Why do not economists talk more about the costs of young people entering adulthood unprepared either for work or citizenship?

Some studies have been done. But the question remains. More work is warranted.

ORGANIZE REGIONAL CADRES

Maybe cadres is not the best word. But it fits. Any group of teachers who has ever contemplated converting an existing school to a teacher-powered status or starting a new school has faced a predictable challenge.

Teachers need assistance in writing and applying for grants—whether directed at foundations or to government agencies—to fund the planning and start-up phases of a new or converted school. Junge knows all this already, because she and her colleagues are constantly helping groups of teachers with their grant-writing and planning. But there are limits to what they can do, with the time and resources available.

Teachers also need legal advice; in every state there are laws about what has to be done and in place to start and operate a school and make it eligible for regular funding.

If the group is not so fortunate as to inherit a facility, they will have to find one, often on the open market. It has to be a building suitable for schooling, or one that can affordably be converted to this use. It has to be in a zone where this is permitted. Often a group of teachers will find it necessary to pay a broker to find this facility.

Some people like budgets. Most teachers though, at least the ones interviewed for this book, need assistance to learn the ropes on finance. They clearly wanted to thoroughly understand the budget. But if teachers are to be in charge, calling the shots, setting the priorities, they must develop a fundamental, ongoing grasp of budget resources. They have to know confidently how much money they can spend each year and on what. There are professionals in any region who can get teachers ready for this responsibility. And people that teachers can hire to do the work they do not want to do.

Then there is governance. How many schools have hit the skids because teachers, eager to be in charge, did not have adequate sophistication about how to make decisions on behalf of the school? This is a challenge that the teacher-powered movement faces all the time, says Junge. Sometimes the law requires that there be a board of directors, or at least a governing council. How is responsibility split? How does one preserve the teacher dominance of the school if there is a board or council making governance decisions?

In all these cases and more, there are professionals in every region who are both sympathetic to these challenges and knowledgeable about teaching others the fundamentals. They often provide *pro bono* assistance, but someone has to find these human resources.

Finally, there are various business operations that have to be done, regardless of how the school is organized or governed. Laws affecting human resources have to be well known and compliance is not optional but expected. And people have to be paid—employees or partners, vendors who provide services, others. Someone has to attend to all this, and the way it is organized makes a big difference in the headache-quotient that teachers report.

Once again, this can be done, in this case, region by region. The model has been tested in the Minneapolis-St. Paul region and it works, leading there to creating a special hybrid co-op that offers services and has members. And the national network can do much of this work too. But either requires resources. If those were available, it is easy to see how the movement might get bigger, faster.

CAMPAIGN FOR GRANTS

In each state where the movement takes root, there are enormous barriers to starting something new, even if that is only converting an existing school inside an operating and willing school district.

Interviewing teachers who have endured this experience, however happily, is to invite many tales of burn-out, of too much work and too little time, of life choices every week. It is no surprise that a major barrier to growth in this movement is that teachers who would normally dive into the work have jobs that take most of their time and energy.

The reality is that, if the movement is to grow any faster, especially in the district sector, teachers who say they want to be in charge have to have the time for planning and the support for the start-up phase of converting a school or starting a new one. That takes money. And they have to get their autonomies in writing.

A few years ago activists succeeded in getting a small grant program enacted by the Minnesota Legislature. It was enough money to support the planning of just a handful of schools. But the funds quickly dried up, exhausted by more demand than supply.

Which reveals another major sticking point: grants, if they are needed, have to see a longer runway than a year or two. Most new schools, even conversion schools, take at least that long to get to an approval point. Then, a different kind of work begins—finding the right teachers, getting a facility, nailing down the best estimates for a budget, dealing with whatever the governance arrangement is, plus negotiating more than most teachers imagine with the state bureaucracy charged with overseeing the entire universe of education.

Public servants, even the best ones, are not known for their friendliness toward risk. They are likely to be skeptics. And they will have many questions at every stage of development. It is reasonable to expect the whole process to take longer. The grant support should contemplate realistically the timeline most new schools face.

Clearly, this is fertile ground for philanthropy. But from whatever source, teachers who want to call the shots and take charge of whole schools have to have financial support for the time it takes to plan the school and get it going.

OPEN UP THE SYSTEM

The mindset problem just keeps coming up. Much of the resistance to a more open system comes from peoples' memories about what they considered to be real school. Anything that looks new or different is suspect. This policy persistence is something Tim McDonald, now working at RAND, recalls seeing in the work of political scientist Eric Patashnik. In Patashnik's work, he finds people just sticking to ideas (like real school) no matter what is proposed as progress.

But there are some policies that could be changed. The lack of portability in retirement programs, as one good example, is a big barrier for many teachers who say they would like to help plan and start a new school and be in charge. "If retirement benefits were portable," McDonald says, "just imagine the change in mobility of people." Actually, nearly everyone knows someone who will freely confess they feel stuck with the employer they have, simply because of the benefit package. The same is true for educators, and retirement programs are the biggest of the barriers.

Obviously, if the dominant district system saw itself as a provider of a good education for kids, not as an operator of schools, the whole scene might change. Education as an industry would then have a chance of changing and improving the way other successful industries have done. They would be self-improving organisms. Today they look increasingly inert, incapable of doing or being anything they think the public would not regard as real school.

But the retirement issue, critical to many teachers who are in the system and do not want to walk away from it, can be solved. Technically, it is easy. Politically, it may be difficult, as associations representing various constituencies within the industry posed their objections.

Morally, though, what is the objection to a teacher staying in a retirement system and teaching in a different kind of school? Districts should be interested in innovation, in experimentation, in having a diverse group of schools. Where they do not, where they seek to standardize everything in sight, where they brook no deviation from central authority, citizens should begin to ask the obvious tough questions.

A good first step: support legislation that allows teachers to stay in their retirement system, with their contributions and the employers going into the same fund.

Then there are the school boards that control what districts do. To offer just one example, in 2009 the Minnesota Legislature, responding to an unusual coalition of unions and business, passed an amendment to its education statutes. This amendment essentially laid out a process for what could be teacher-powered schools. (It called them "self-governed.") That was a decade ago. No district has used this amendment. In some cases, the union was cool to the idea, in others, it has been the board; result, nothing has happened. Clearly, it does not pay to set up something like the United Nations Security Council, where any nation's veto means nothing happens. If legislatures are indeed the policymakers for the education industry, lawmakers should make real decisions. Decisions that do not depend on agreements that are guaranteed to prove elusive. And the system continues to resist change.

CHANGE TEACHER PREPARATION—PLEASE

Nothing begs for change more than teacher preparation programs. Optimists point to the Relay Graduate Education School, which grew out of the charter movement and looks quite different. Or High Tech High's Graduate School of Education, designed originally to be different and prepare a different kind of teacher.

But a small number of exceptions proves the general rule: most teacher preparation programs have stayed mostly the same. Walter Enloe, a retired professor at the Hamline Graduate School of Education in Saint Paul, says it succinctly. "The system is the problem," as he puts it. So obviously schools of education do not change much; "they were not designed to change."

In his book *The Global Achievement Gap* Tony Wagner confesses that "what one has to do to become a teacher or administrator is nearly identical to what students have to do for a high school diploma—take a disjointed collection of courses of uneven quality and then pass tests that rarely measure the skills that matter most."

Federal data from the National Center for Education Statistics imply that fewer young people these days want to be teachers. Enrollment has dropped in some states over the last decade by as much as 50 percent, with an average drop of 30 percent across all schools of education. Traditional programs actually lost 43 percent of their expected new enrollment. But alternatives that were not affiliated with any college or university saw increases of 42 percent.

Back in 2005 Arthur Levine, then president of Teachers College at Columbia University authored a report in which he said teacher preparation programs ranged from "inadequate to appalling." That same year the National Council on Teacher Quality called schools of education an "industry of mediocrity."

Kate Walsh, who has been doggedly tracking whether teacher preparation programs in existing schools of education are doing a good job (she finds most are not), is the president of the National Council on Teacher Quality. She quickly dismisses the notion that teacher leadership could be taught in today's programs. "Look around," she suggests, "and you may find some teacher leadership courses, but there are a lot of competing interests on teacher professional development (which comes later)."

Joe Nathan, one of the pioneers responsible for the introduction of chartering in the United States, takes a dim view of what colleges of education provide these days. He says:

> One of the mistakes of the alternative school and chartered movement has been the failure to figure out how we can influence and be heavily involved in preparation of the next generation of teachers and school leaders. So people being trained to enter the field heard nothing, or mostly negative things about these ideas from colleges of education. And many colleges of education faculty have contributed to negative research on both alternative and chartered public schools.

The Bush Foundation (named for an original executive of 3M, not a U.S. president), headquartered in Saint Paul, Minnesota, initiated an effort back in 2008 to get colleges of education in the colleges and universities of Minnesota and South and North Dakota to change their practices.

However worthwhile the objective, the results were marginal. Some institutions did begin to see customers when school districts were mentioned. And some tightened their recruitment standards. And a few added courses. But most participating institutions stuck with their steadily evolving but largely unchanged curricular and program practices.

One pioneer not surprised by what he sees is Doug Thomas, who worked to forge a new kind of school in rural Henderson, Minnesota. When he opened the MNCS a quarter century ago, many teachers were dumbfounded to find themselves in charge. And Thomas blames the popular assumptions on teacher preparation as it is practiced in most colleges of education. "Those places have become revenue machines for their institutions," he says, and "besides, existing institutions have a hard time changing very much."

That would not surprise the late Clayton Christensen, the longtime Harvard Business School professor, whose signature theory about disruptive innovation still finds incumbent organizations clinging to their cherished operating models. Established organizations, Christensen maintains, just have great difficulty making any real change in their ways of doing things. Even if they want to. Even if there is serious money on the table. Even when they see the upstarts threatening to replace them in the market.

That premise played out perfectly when Larry Rosenstock started High Tech High in San Diego early in this century. He was starting a different kind of school, using technology as a tool but offering a totally different culture than the standard school. Rosenstock was soon frustrated that he could not find new teachers who had the preparation for the kind of school he was trying to build. He was looking for people passionate about their disciplines but confident enough to do whatever worked to get results with kids. He was looking for people who would design their way to results. He had no interest in telling teachers how to teach.

So Rosenstock labored for about a decade, leaning into the California Assembly culture, until he finally emerged with the authority to start what is now the High Tech High Graduate School of Education.

Maybe they exist, but it is not easy to find any existing traditional school of education that prepares people for the teaching of the future, a future in which teachers will act more like coaches than instructors, will help to design the learning experience, not imagine themselves to be the whole source. Schools of education will need to prepare people to be professionals, fully in charge of what matters in their work.

There is scant evidence that this is happening. Just take one example: The College of Education at the University of Texas in its winter 2020 magazine recalls several months in which faculty, staff, and students worked on a new vision and signature areas to emphasize. The new vision suggested a "transformation of education." In an interview with Dean Charles Martinez, he is quoted as saying:

> We have the unique capacity to develop, test, and implement interventions that can lead to lasting changes for students and schools. Moreover, in our academic programs we have the unique responsibility to train education and health professionals and leaders who are capable of interrupting the factors that impede student success, and to realign the system to serve all kids.

Sounds all right, even if it reads stilted and academic. But there is nothing in what followed that suggested anyone understood what "transformational" meant or any sense of how any of this might be done. No strategy.

Relay Graduate School of Education—now with branches all over the United States—comes closer than most organizations. Its stated mission says "continuous improvement" and puts students at the center. It says it teaches principals to stop trying "to manage school buildings and start inspiring teachers." Well said. Not easy to do. Unless the power shifts and teachers are in charge.

Relay, according to Brent Maddin, a veteran of Relay's staff, who now works for the Mary Lou Fulton College of Education at Arizona State University (ASU) says, "we got it all wrong at traditional schools when we emphasized the individual teachers. We should have been educating people to be collaborators."

And the system we produced? "It's not designed to put the kids first," said Maddin.

Maybe what is going on at ASU will be different. Maddin now heads the Next Generation Workforce effort for the Fulton College of Education at ASU. The language he uses to describe preparation and the relationship of the school to its "customers" is strikingly different. The effort is worth watching, but it is very difficult for colleges of education, producing revenue their institutions need and have come to expect, to make fundamental changes.

Rick Hess and Bruno Manno, concluding their edited book *Customized Schooling*, underscore how few education preparation programs do anything but assume that all potential teachers are indistinguishable. They mention Hunter College in New York City because it caters to teachers in New York. And, along with kudos for High Tech High's new work, they cite the Klingenstein Center at Columbia University for its emphasis on preparation for independent school work.

Those authors also give some credit to the New Teacher Project (NTP). They quote the writing of Joe Williams, who says NTP swoops in to meet needs "not met by traditional talent recruitment methods." And Teach for America has generated abundant controversy over its boot-camp approach, while remaining rather popular for getting bright young graduates into classrooms.

But consider how many education shops there are, all over the country. If so few are trying to change, what does that say? Meanwhile, more new teachers are pouring into the system, expecting what they do not find.

Chapter 5

Rocks in the Road
Getting Past Obstacles

The teacher-powered movement is growing. Those who have been in its leadership are now spread out over twenty states. Those ambassadors are passionate, persuasive emissaries for the movement. Every time there is a national gathering, EE has to cut off registration, because demand is higher than hotel capacity.

The enthusiasm one feels at these national gatherings is palpable. Even though most conference attendees start out knowing only a few people, most seem to meet new people rapidly. There is an air of camaraderie that is hard to miss. The commitment to the movement shown by these teachers makes the surveys of 2003 and 2013 come alive; it shows what the promise is.

There is no reason to assume that the growth trajectory will not continue or even increase. The movement is badly needed in America, which remains stuck in a mostly early-20th-century model. Many, including this author, are convinced the nation could show the way to a better system by encouraging this growth in schools where teachers call the shots.

So, the road ahead looks clear, except for a few rocks. Going for growth requiring good steering around those rocks. The largest rocks in the road are the threat of a by-pass and pseudo teacher-powered schools that distort the original vision but attract students; many good ideas faded when taken over by people uninterested in the original goal.

THE BY-PASS POSSIBILITY

The rock here is the potential that the system as we have come to know it will simply be "by-passed," and that teachers will not have any more influence than they have today, likely less. Most people in the industry do not consider a by-pass to be a serious threat. Sure, there have been home schools for a long time. And there are those still pushing vouchers, even though the national movement for chartering reduced what was once a growing fervor for private education.

No, the real risk is that if the system continues to buck fundamental change, students, who are rapidly learning in all kinds of new ways, will force change. They will find other avenues and use them. School as we have known it could become irrelevant.

Think that is fanciful? As Kolderie puts it, all society needs are for a few things now murky to become clear:

- Alternative ways to learn just about anything.
- Some entity to validate what students know and can do.
- Acceptance of that validation by next stops—whether college or a job.

Think that is unlikely? Does anyone think young people today do not learn in different ways than previous generations?

In *Disrupting Class* (2008), the authors claimed that half of high school enrollment would be taken online by 2019. That prediction, which seemed plausible at the time, ran into the resistance to change within the system, and the mixed quality of the software industry, which produced some stellar tools and some just so-so. Districts bought both. Reputational damage was inevitable.

But the S-curve is admired for good reason by academics, because time after time, it turns out to correctly track the trajectory of any upstart threat to a dominant incumbent in an industry. The so-called "real schools" are certainly in that target zone.

S-curves basically plot the gradual, then the sudden, substitution of a new way for the old way. It is usually applied to products and industries. But it fits the learning question very well. For some indefinitely period of time, the curve is pretty flat, leading incumbent organizations to think nothing bad is likely to happen to their dominance. Then, almost suddenly, at some inflection point, the "market" for the new way seems to take off. Incumbents are left flabbergasted.

This has happened in nearly every industry. Cameras, computers, and cars. Newspapers, news in all forms, books, films. On and on. What people see as quality, including speed of access, gets better and costs often go down. Given that schooling is an old media approach, why would this not eventually happen to schooling? Ken Auletta, who wrote the book *Googled—The End of the World as We Know It*, responded to a question once about whether school was "old media," having just lectured that old media was essentially toast in view of technological change. Auletta did not pause, but just said, "Yes, it is."

Already, a student can tour the British Museum online and have a better look at everything there without the expense of the trip. A student can learn a language right now with Babbel or Duolingo on the phone. Get a chemistry course, complete with a lab experience, without going to a school and have a high-quality learning experience. Learn a musical instrument. The possibilities are becoming endless and increasingly compelling.

Schools in remote areas are finding they can send students to the library where they can go online and sign up for courses the district cannot afford to offer because of scale.

In traditional schools, which today still enroll most of the students, taking some courses online would have a positive effect on operating costs. And teachers could be associated with those courses and become more like coaches. Most students could take the course by themselves though and do well.

Just look at what happened in photography. Many adults today grew up in a world in which cameras seemed to get better every year. Film came out with higher resolution; lens became sharper, more flexible; cameras showed a variety of shapes and sizes and with a dazzling array of functions.

Then in 1975, engineers and scientists in Kodak labs in New York figured out how to capture images without film, in essence the precursor to the digital camera. Excited to show the potential of their discovery, they presented it to company executives who were not, to put it mildly, amused. They reminded the scientists that Kodak as a "film company." So why would anyone at Kodak be interested in a product that did not need film? The rest is history.

If an S-curve of how young people learn does mature, before teachers have regained control over classrooms, even entire schools, teachers as we know them may become collaterally obsolete—somewhat like film—needing to fundamentally change their roles. And who knows what artificial intelligence will mean for schooling? The by-pass of the traditional school risks inevitability and certainly appears unstoppable. This would be a big rock in the road.

Many insiders do not think the "district" as a piece of American democracy can last much longer. Charles Kerchner of Claremont College wrote an entire book on *Learning from L.A.*, which was really about the slow but sure implosion of the district. Some speakers on the circuit talk openly about a "post-district" scene in the United States. One teacher interviewed for this book said that he "would not bet on the district where he works lasting more than three years." "It simply is not designed to help kids learn. It's designed for adult employment," he said, pretty bluntly.

If districts begin to fail in large numbers, and more teachers discover the professional option of being in charge, then no matter whether philanthropy notices or other big money comes or does not come, there will be change.

Districts are increasingly aware that they need to change. Scarcely an issue goes by but that *Education Week* has an article about districts in distress. Writer Daarel Burnett II in "Why Don't Struggling K-12 Districts Just Dissolve?," says there are "about 13,500 school districts in the country, and a growing number are in fiscal distress because of rising pension and health care costs and dwindling tax revenue after precipitous drops in student enrollment." It may get worse.

Paul Hill and his colleagues at the Center for Reinventing Public Education have long pushed districts to reposition themselves to manage large portfolios—all the schools in their area. But not try to operate any of them directly. That is very difficult for districts, particularly for boards, whose members regularly run for election on what they will do if they are running the schools.

Large bureaucracies are another problem. One superintendent was a visitor in another U.S. city and, after making his presentation, was taken to the central office of one of the larger districts in the state. He discovered it had about the same number of students he did back home. But when he asked how many people worked in the central office, he was told, "Oh, about 500." He now thinks he was less than diplomatic. In fact, he was then merely blunt, telling his guide that as long as this many people depended on telling others what to do, it just was not reasonable to expect much change. And this was a district losing enrollment every year, year after year.

Then 2020 saw the effects of a pandemic on just about every enterprise. Schools were mostly closed. Learning went online. Most districts, it appears from reporting, tried to replicate what was happening in classrooms online. Many kids said they were bored. Some did not show up at all. Newspapers and blogs wrote about online being a poor substitute for being at school. For students with special needs, the change was certainly traumatic; they needed contact with professionals. Many students reported, not surprisingly, that they missed the social contact with their friends.

What if enough students discovered the plethora of software long available, much of it very good in a variety of subjects? What if students who long struggled with school as it is organized today found they did much better working independently. Will district staff begin to use the technology? Will they, as Sal Khan repeatedly suggests, pick two or three pieces of software and just a variety of specialized courses and begin weaving those into schooling? Who knows? There are small signs of this happening, but not much.

Districts are remarkable for their resistance to changing anything truly fundamental. So, if one assumes little or no change in districts, growing the movement, while respecting its grassroots, is probably doable provided that there is a national network that supports the teachers who are taking the risks and provides the kind of development backing that the Center for

Collaborative Education has long given to the pilot schools in Boston and later Los Angeles. Remember what Dan French said: "Without the CCE, the pilot schools would never have survived."

But they did. And the teachers in teacher-powered schools have such a network. And an organization (EE) thoroughly committed to careful management.

THE MOVEMENT GETS DISTORTED

Some who want the teacher-powered movement to succeed are wary. They observed what happened to the chartering idea. It was supposed to be an innovative way to start a new school; and it was assumed that new schools would explore new possibilities for methods and learning approaches, from which other schools in the dominant K–12 system would learn. And to some degree, and in some cities, this has happened.

But, alongside good results has been a trend to think of a chartered school as a *type* of school. Even researchers now engaged in the spurious practice of comparing results in charters with traditional public schools. And the dominant districts began seeing chartering as competition, rather than a research-and-development laboratory.

Chartering, as a strategy to spur innovation in public schools, passed first in Minnesota in 1991. Though it was a surprise to most education watchers, many states over the next few years passed laws authorizing chartered schools. Within a decade, it was most states.

Quite naturally, a national association was formed, started by Jon Schroeder, who had been a staffer for then U.S. senator David Durenberger. The senator from Minnesota had played a key role in lining up federal support for charter start-ups. Schroder created something called Charter Friends National Network. That eventually led to something more formal, the National Charter Schools Alliance, intended to be a member organization of state associations and supporters across the states.

But in the early 2000s, large foundations and companies got interested and seemed to take control, with their money. They insisted, as Kolderie wrote, "not on a membership organization, but a leadership organization." It would be called the National Association for Public Charter Schools (now popularly called the National Alliance). And the director brought in, Nelson Smith, at a meeting at Mackinac Island in Michigan, said the mission was for the sector to grow by doing traditional school better, demonstrating accountability for achievement, conventionally defined. Some criticize the foundations that had been supportive of what they now called inadequate. But it was clearly their money and their decision to make, says Howard Fuller, former superintendent in Milwaukee and now with the University of Marquette; Fuller was supposed to be the chair of the new board.

Rather quickly, there followed the establishment of the National Association of Charter School Authorizers to set standards. Authorizing improved where it was weakest. As scaling up became the thing to do, there appeared the New Schools Venture Fund and the Charter Schools Growth Fund, which would promote more entrepreneurial approaches but also big organizations that would handle multiple schools. Some of these Charter Management Organizations (CMOs) worked well, but they also became quite controversial as it became clear that many were for-profit organizations; people suspected they made too many decisions based on money rather than the best interests of kids.

Back in Minnesota, people like Senator Ember Reichgott Junge (no relation to Amy Junge), who was a lead Minnesota legislator in passing the nation's first chartering law, and Nathan—both worried that the movement was losing its bearings, straying from what its founders envisioned as the role for chartering. Kolderie, agreeing that accountability was good, would write in *Thinking Out the How*: "Accountability for what? For achievement, certainly. What achievement? English and math only? Assessment only to measure proficiency on state exams?"

Kolderie himself does not see the movements of teacher-powered schools and chartered schools as comparable situations. He is not so worried that teacher-powered schools will lose their sense of original mission. And the National Alliance for Public Charter Schools is on the record as supporting a wider view of assessment than just state exams.

But Lars Esdal, who is the executive director of EE, which manages the national movement, puts his mild warning in these terms: "The teacher-powered idea is like a van trucking down the highway of positive educational change." What Esdal does not want to see is the movement joining other promises of transformation change in what Tony Bryk, in his book *Learning to Improve*, called "the chronic failure of reform ideas."

So as the movement goes down the highway of promises, Esdal says, and over the past five years, "You could have seen several snazzy-looking reform cars go zipping past us, ten times as fast. These cars had fresh paint jobs, souped-up engines, and loads of foundation gas in their tanks."

Before you know it, though, he goes on, "You start to see, the smoldering wreckage of these good ideas alongside the road. They were going too fast, lost control, and spun right into the guardrails." Who's going to see them as legitimate anymore, he wonders.

So, the risk is, in Esdal's thinking, that teacher-powered schools "get scaled," rather than "scaling themselves." He is not against more rapid growth. He sees the need for it, but his thinking is sobering advice that enthusiasts should "push the limits, but respect the teacher-led authenticity of the movement."

To be fair, other voices chimed in with concern too. Erik Berg, vice president of the Boston Teachers Union also worries "if the movement goes too rapidly to scale, it may be hijacked." Another officer in that union who has been an ambassador for the movement, Taryn Snyder, almost completely captures the ambivalence of some people. She says, "The movement needs to grow, particularly for the many teachers who don't even know this is an option for them, but it shouldn't grow too fast."

"Hijacked" was a term also used by Albert Shanker, who in the 1980s flirted with the charter idea and saw it as a path to real professionalism for teachers. In Richard Kahlenberg's biography of Shanker, he quotes him as watching "with alarm as the concept he'd put forward began to move away from the public school reform effort."

Once private corporations got into the chartering business, Shanker became sure that the movement had been taken over, and not in a good way, though in 1995 he was so supportive of chartering that he told a congressman working on D.C.'s chartering policy that every school should be a charter. But Shanker was surely against for-profit chartering.

Junge supports growth, but warns that "the power of the movement is its grassroots. So, while scaling is easy if everything's the same, everything is not the same in this movement. Each school is different."

Junge remembers too what she thinks happened to chartering. She says that "in the quest for growth and scalability, the chartering concept was diluted to the point of barely resembling Shanker's idea." She does not think that will happen to the teacher-powered movement.

Asked once whether he would be open to replicating High Tech High in San Diego beyond its multischool campus there, with its famously persistent waiting lists, founder Rosenstock politely demurred. He too knows every school is different. That every school reflects a different culture, a different setting. Big Picture Schools founder Eliot Washor used to lament the pressure from funders to replicate these schools in different cities. It was very difficult to do, he often said.

The point is not that replicating success is bad, but that it is hard. And that explains why there is so much variation within teacher-powered schools. Every one of them is different, by design. Innovation should be the goal, rather than mere replication; finding out what works best for this school in that situation—that's the goal.

Kerchner, who's written books and endless articles about schools, particularly focused on the labor dimension, when asked about the potential for growth in the teacher-powered schools, said,

Well, I haven't thought about this for a while, I'll admit. But I think that teachers by and large are smarter than the organizations in which they work. There are various ways you can recognize and encourage teacher smarts. Start with the premise that teachers have talent. But teachers don't have language that describes this talent. Because they work in the organizations they are working in—essentially industrial work—with someone else designing and evaluation of the work. They've never been required to develop a language system. They may have to now.

A language that fits teacher-powered schools, yes. But they also need scale. And that only happens with growth. Toch, who is also been watching the ups and downs of education's fortunes for a long time, now says, "Scale, even in our radically decentralized system, is everything. 150 schools, that's nothing. 7000 charter schools—now that's the beginning of serious scale. Don't scale, and you're just a drop in the bucket."

So the pressure is on. And if there is turmoil and failure and everything is up for grabs, teachers may be the only survivors, ready or not. In which case, teachers unions matter even more than they do today. And the dilemma of teachers unions is the subject of the next chapter.

Chapter 6

First Bird Off the Wire
Bargaining for What Future?

Remember NEA's John Wright's question in a previous chapter? It was a good question. What if young people disillusioned with what career teaching looks like to them discover the teacher-powered movement? What if they find they could have full control over what mattered for school and student success? What might they do?

Much of the answer depends on what large teacher unions do, propelled by the demand from local chapters and eventually from state-level teacher union organizations. The teacher unions are large. The NEA alone comes close to one in every one hundred Americans. The AFT is smaller but more politically active. They may not have control or conduct collective bargaining in some states, but they leave big footprints wherever they go. If they were to get behind the teacher-powered movement, seeing it as a way to advance the professional status of their members, much would change. If just one of them, willing even not eager to be the first birds to fly off the wire, they would find audiences they never knew they had.

Most authors writing about making schools better have made the darkest assumptions about any assistance from teacher unions. In fact, most books characterize these unions as a major obstacle blocking change, sometimes even the enemy. Terry Moe and John Chubb published an entire book and stirred a major controversy in 1990. They painted the teachers unions as a main obstacle to needed change.

Terry Moe was a Stanford University professor. He continued to write critically of the unions. In 2011, he said in *Special Interests* that unions, while "the most powerful force in American education," use their muscle to "promote their own special interests at the expense of what is best for kids."

Do the teachers unions sometimes take refuge behind the interests of the kids? Sure. But one wonders whether Moe and others have thought about what caused the unions to be so combative? What caused them to feel like teachers needed protection? There may be good reasons why unions behave the way they do.

Still some, once the potential of unions is mentioned, immediately cite Mexico's teachers unions as what might happen—unions becoming bosses, determining hiring and firing, taking over the system for their own benefit—not caring about the kids.

But notwithstanding the chorus of critics, anyone serious about launching publicity big enough to make teachers all across the United States aware of this professional option would have to think about the communications vehicle of the unions. The unions might be thought of as a massive but unmobilized army for change. That is a big thought. A risky bet, many would say.

But it does not take long if the question gets asked, to discover that inside of many teacher unions—whether one of the two large national organizations, the NEA or the AFT, or a state organization or a local chapter where there is teacher-powered activity underway—there is at least the beginning of an argument.

That argument, which most often takes a polite form (but not always), is mostly between the traditionalists, who worry about anything that departs from the structure of collective bargaining agreements and people inside unions who see a different future—one that supports teachers who want to opt for full responsibility for schools.

You can almost hear the conversation. The traditionalist, usually an older teacher, is saying, "This is a dangerous proposition. It colors outside the lines of our agreements. It undermines everything we have worked so long to gain. We have to ignore it, hope it goes away. All this stuff is management's problem."

Then the other voices speak up. "Yes," they say, "but these teachers in so-called teacher-powered schools, have achieved almost overnight what we have labored for decades on and couldn't get—either through legislation or bargaining. They are now in charge of what matters in schools. How can we possibly be against that?"

These arguments are not new but the patience of many is wearing thin. As long ago as 1997, the new president of the NEA, Bob Chase, made a memorable speech to the members of the National Press Club. He called for "a new unionism," one that made the union a "partner" rather than a steady adversary. He was not given up on bargaining for better wages or working conditions, but he wanted to improve the quality of teaching.

Chase would go on to make friends across lines and try to re-do the massive organization he headed. But the Chase legacy is today a sad reminder of how difficult change can be in a democratically governed institution. He never stopped trying though.

Just imagine that next year the head of one of the big teachers' unions were to make this speech:

This may be my final word to all of you. That you can decide with your votes. But today I am going to say what is on my mind, and in my heart, without any concern for how popular I am with you or anyone else. When I ran for this office, I said I would tell you the truth, always. Today I am going to prove it. At whatever cost.

I firmly believe that our union is at one of those crossroads we are often talking about or making the subject of some conference. A long time ago—or at least it seems like a long time ago—our predecessors faced a somewhat similar dilemma. As charters emerged as viable alternatives and as the monopoly receded—yes I know, many of you do not like that term, but it is what we had—our union had a choice between, as a now retired academic who spent his career studying unions as well as education put it, "trench warfare or a transformational vision." We chose warfare. And we have been waging it, more or less, for decades.

Sure, the passage of No Child Left Behind, and the blaming directed at teachers that followed, put us squarely on the defensive. We've fought back. As we should.

But as we have fought NCLB, charters and later testing and the more recent assaults on anything associated with unions, we have made few gains. Sure, we are still powerful, but I would say less respected. We are seen as just another interest group protecting its members. We do that well. But that is all we do.

I would claim that we are fortunate. Fortunate because we do have choices. We have decisions to make. There is more than one path that a national teachers union could take. And they are very different. We could continue what we have been doing: fighting anything and anyone who says or does anything we think is inconsistent with total support of our agenda. Or, if we choose to—and it would take a lot of courage to do it because most of our members seem to want us to stay the course—we could announce that we are going to become a truly professional organization. That we will support teachers in transforming the very core of what constitutes good preparation; that will be bad news for hundreds of colleges with teacher preparation programs populated by professors who do not want anything to change. But we could say that.

We might also say that, even as we continue to represent teachers for bargaining with districts, we want to break through longstanding barriers and argue for giving teachers the autonomy to work together and make decisions that strengthen the schools and the schools and families they serve. That's right. We could make a big deal out of the school being the unit that matters, the platform for success for students.

Oh, I know what many of you are saying to yourselves: Don't we already say that? Isn't that a part of a platform? Yes, but I'm saying we need to really mean this when we say it. Make it mean something real.

As we learned in the pandemic that broke out in 2020, school is more than a place. It is a process of learning to learn. It is a challenge to individual students to find what they care about most and learn what they need to know about that, as well as be an educated person. We learned that kids have to be motivated in order to learn. It is our job to find the tools, lift up the best strategies, to unlock that motivation for kids who are very different from each other. More different even than previous generations. The point is that schooling is not what it used to be.

Yes, I know, we all carry around the notion of what 'real school' is—or maybe was. It is not the same. And it has not been for a long time. The kids knew it before we did. School is a process for learning—wherever it may happen or however it takes place. The role of the teacher is more like a coach, who learns how to get the best each person has to give, who insists on practice to get better, who realizes that each person is different and respects that difference.

I am aware of the arguments going on in state teacher union organizations. It has been, where it happens, between those who think we should support teachers having more authority—even total control over what matters to school and student success—and those who are fearful that teachers in charge of schools is just a passing trend, that it will go away, and we will look foolish for supporting the idea, and that we would be better off investing our attention and resources to protect what we've won over the years.

I may be proved wrong, but I do not believe what is now called 'teacher-powered' schools is a passing fancy. The idea is not going away. It is growing—and it should grow. Think about it: these teachers, now in over half the states with the number of such schools growing every year, have achieved what we were never able to get through legislation or bargaining. They have real authority over their work. They control what matters for school and student success.

Just look at their retention numbers. The comparison with most schools—and the districts they are part of—is embarrassing. Teachers clearly like teacher-powered schools because they stay in them. Even if they report they are working harder and longer than before. Even if they are violating work rules we bargained hard to get for most teachers.

I am asking you today: why would we ignore this idea? And why would we ever think of opposing it? Why would we not support any group of teachers who says they are ready to be in charge of schools?

So, that is what I am telling you. If you vote for me for another term, this is what I will work on: to make our union one that welcomes this change, one that supports teacher groups who want to change their school and are willing to be accountable for results. Will we continue to represent people who want the traditional collective bargaining agreement. Certainly. As long as there is demand for it and circumstances make it necessary.

But I do foresee a day when traditional bargaining will seem as obsolete as a dial-up telephone. I see a day when students are learning partially online and partially in groups, all coordinated by teachers working in collaborative environments that might seem chaotic to traditionalists but make good sense to those involved. I see a day when colleges of education prepare teachers to be fully professional. I see a day when districts, if they exist at all, are managing selection and evaluation of schools, not operating any of them. I see a day when it will be hard to become a teacher but a lot more satisfying to be one. I see a day when teachers are seen by society as up there with doctors and lawyers, maybe a bit above them in respect and even compensation.

I may not live to see all that. But I do know what steps we have to take to get there. And I am prepared to lead, prepared to take this union in that direction. If you will let me. Thank you.

In a post-Janus world—now jargon all too familiar to everyone in unions—expectations and assumptions are undergoing radical review. And it is not merely the Janus decision driving change, it is everything else that has changed the reality, altered the conditions in which the union and its educators operate.

Today, as previously mentioned, nearly half of all teachers, according to the latest PDK polling data, want more say about teaching conditions. And even though they say they would strike to get higher wages, slightly over half the teachers polled want more say about the standards of a school, about testing policies and what is in the curriculum.

Peggy Brookins, who heads the National Board for Professional Teaching Standards, noted in a recent podcast that upwards of 90 percent of physicians have been board certified. She wonders why teachers cannot be at 90 percent too.

Then there is the current (2020) case just concluded through which the U.S. Supreme Court has changed the eligibility of scholarship money to all kinds of schools, including those with religious affiliations. Thirty-eight states have constitutional amendments (so-called Blaine amendments, named for the 19th-century Maine congressman who tried to get this provision into the U.S. Constitution), prohibiting the use of public money for sectarian or religious schooling. At the time, there was rampant sentiment arrayed against Catholic schools. There seems little question that unions find this news, if unsurprising given the current makeup of the Supreme Court, unsettling.

And union-watchers should pay more attention to the software industry. Having disrupted everything else in sight, how long will it be before its products break up what is left of the monopoly that schools have enjoyed over the education of children? This is at the heart of the potential by-pass mentioned in the previous chapter.

School is still seen as a place, but for how long? Learning now takes place in so many forms and forums. Certainly not just in school. Some current students, like Lincoln Bacal, a 2020 senior at Venture Academy in Minneapolis, who says her experience with (unionized) public schools was mostly "how effective they are in crushing every entrepreneurial instinct students have."

That seems harsh, but her statement is not far off from what many current students say about what they know as school.

There is little question these days that unions have declined. Last year employers added over 2 million new jobs. Union membership went down by 170,000, continuing a decade-long trend. Today, there are 14.6 million union workers or barely 10 percent of the workforce. The only bright spot for unions is the public sector, where nearly a third of union members hold jobs at the federal, state or local level, including teachers.

Yet, there is scant discussion of what unions could do that is different. The unions could, should, must get on the road to different or they will be increasingly irrelevant to what matters in American's lives.

Does it not feel like people now live in a world of greatly accelerated change? The pandemic and then the uprisings of long-simmering racial unrest, have added to this feeling. Especially for those who live in urban areas or who are swimming in the vast sea of media commentary or social media posts, it seems like everything is changing all the time. Norms are just traditions to discard. Values are fungible. Past experience is a poor guide to future expectations.

And for people in the relatively quiet areas of the country, who have experienced less change, there is a palpable feeling of being left behind. Discarded. Ignored. Not valued.

Apparently, many teachers feel the same way. In the spring of 2019, Randi Weingarten, the longtime head of the AFT, appeared at the National Press Club. According to coverage in *Education Week*, she saturated her comments with sad references to the deteriorated conditions of work, saying that "deprofessionalization is killing the soul of teaching."

Weingarten hammered the point repeatedly, saying that teachers "are no longer seen as professionals." She described them as micromanaged, forced to focus on standardized tests, and denied the freedom to teach.

Art Wise, the former longtime head of the National Council for the Accreditation of Teacher Education (later to merge with a similar organization and become the Council for the Accreditation of Educator Preparation) and chair of the Center of Teaching Quality board, who has tracked both unions and the industry itself for a long time, argues that "any real change will have to come from the bottom up." He also points out that there are no real professions that put new people into unsupervised situations right away. Only education.

Some take hope from seeing that the AFT was supportive of the formation of the Guild. The Guild was formed in 2011 shortly after the Minnesota Legislature approved another slot for a single-purpose authorizer. And the founder was Louise Sundin, who by then had left the presidency of the Minneapolis Federation of Teachers (MFT). Both she and her successor at MFT, Lynn Nordgren, were weary of watching every gain in the Minneapolis schools neutralized by administrations bent on keeping centralized control. Every effort at helping teachers exercise professional control over their work was stymied.

Today Nordgren, now retired from the MFT, is the chair of the Guild's board. The authorizer's portfolio is increasingly full of teacher-powered schools. Nordgren and Sundin both were and are union stalwarts, but also they were keenly aware that many parents of minority kids were desperately looking for any alternative for their children. Sundin now thinks that unions got on the wrong side of the charter question early on. Had they been more involved, they might have had more influence over what kinds of schools emerged.

The Guild got more than one grant from the AFT, significant financial support for new schools that would be more responsive to parents and community. Nordgren is clear about AFT support and she does not believe Randi Weingarten, the longtime president of the AFT, has a serious issue with charters, though it seems clear Weingarten does not like charter management organizations with a profit motive. "But she supported the Guild all the way," Nordgren pointed out.

The Guild continues to push the teacher-powered idea. And getting results. It is a union invention that is working. The state union has so far ignored the Guild. And the local union shifts back and forth, for and against the Guild.

Remember, the idea for teachers having more influence actually originated with people like the late Albert Shanker, the longtime head of the AFT. Many decades ago, when Eric Premack, now in California, heading a development organization that helps charter schools, was a graduate student at the University of Chicago, he made a cold call to Albert Shanker's office. He had heard that Shanker was showing up for a speech in Chicago and he wanted some time with him. Amazingly, Shanker took him to lunch and among the many candid things Premack recalls is Shanker's description of how much American education was now like a drowning man clinging to a rock in the Rubicon, uncertain of how to save himself. Perhaps the scene looks better now, but probably not. And that was a long time ago.

Today unions devoted to teachers are still troubled and besieged organizations but the opportunities are also still there. Either or both of them could become champions for professionalism and could provide serious leadership for a national movement of teachers in charge of what matters in schools.

The accountability agenda remains strong. Why not leverage that public sentiment and invite a new deal for teachers—more authority and more accountability? That is essentially what Graba told members of TURN long ago. It is still true.

It was Shanker who famously said, "If you want to hold teachers accountable, then teachers have to be able to run the school."

The teacher-powered movement does enjoy considerable teacher union support in places like New York and Boston. If teachers unions in more places were to get in front of this movement, rather than chasing it from behind, the movement would grow. But to be a player, at least one of the unions has to show the courage and vision to fly off the wire of the status quo.

Chapter 7

Conclusion

The teacher-powered idea may be the only fundamental change in schooling that will spread and last. Nothing else has. And while the debate continues over how fast it should grow, grow it will. It is too good an idea not to spread. Enthusiasm for it, especially among those who have tasted its fruit personally, is impressive. Students in these schools are engaged and motivated. Results are better when teachers have real influence, as a growing body of academic research clearly shows.

Growth may take time though. A former prime minister of Great Britain, Benjamin Disraeli, once said that "genius was prolonged patience." That advice may point to what preserves this movement—patience loaded up with a heavy dose of perseverance. Because the resistance to change is not going away.

THE SYSTEM AND ITS GRAMMAR

It was David Tyack and Larry Cuban in their 1995 book *Tinkering Toward Utopia* who used the term "grammar" to describe the implicit rules that govern the structure of schooling in America. The most common question adults ask kids today, when they first meet, is "what grade are you in?"

Taken from Prussia in the mid-19th century, this basic grammar, with its cornerstone DNA in what is now thought of as age-grading, is the foundation for the real school mindset. Tyack and Cuban wrote that "little has changed in the way schools divide time and space, classify students and allocate them into classrooms, splinter knowledge into 'subjects,' and award grades and 'credits' as evidence of learning." It was merely a "product of history," they wrote, "not some primordial creation."

But age-grading is so sticky that even in New Orleans, where there was a nearly total replacement of schools and most of them being chartered after Hurricane Katrina in 2005, this structure still dominates schools.

In the early 20th century, the system embraced the Carnegie credit. Henry Pritchett, who was then president of the Carnegie Foundation for the Advancement of Teaching, started defining credit as a unit earned by a course of five periods a week for an academic year. That was 1905.

In late 1906, the presidents of several elite universities gathered at Andrew Carnegie's mansion in New York city and substantially embraced the Carnegie Unit as the answer to what they saw as chaos and disarray in school structures. The one-room schoolhouse was long gone in most parts of America, but there was too much differentiation, they thought. So, Carnegie, though he had established a foundation originally to provide pensions for retiring university professors, is best remembered today partly for the historic chain of libraries, but also for this way of keeping score in schools. Once accrediting agencies got on board, the Carnegie Unit was integrated into the permanent structure of schooling.

And the prevalence of this model is not restricted to the United States. As Cuban posted in a spring blog in 2019, this structure for schooling exists in most of Europe, in Asia and Africa, and Latin America.

Age-grading and the Carnegie Unit combined to make schooling a platform for predictable success for some young people, but turned schools into factories of failure for many other students, who had other interests or needed more time or learned another way.

Except for sports. In sports, if a tennis athlete is extremely good at the game, they might be named to the varsity team, even if that student were only a freshman in school. There are cases in which kids in middle school have landed on varsity teams, because they were talented and ready. Why do not we do the same thing in algebra, many ask? In sports, it matters what you know and can do, regardless of where you have been, how you are classified, or what academic record you have compiled.

But in school, teachers have to follow a certain pace in their classes. Introduction to Biology must be taught and learned in one semester. Since most schools have to cover certain subjects each year, it follows that teachers will necessarily be scuba-diving, not doing any deep dives on anything. Like the bus analogy in an earlier chapter suggests, if a teacher spends a lot of time on one dimension of a subject, something else has to give. That is efficient, but perhaps not very effective for most students.

Every known effort to break this real school paradigm and substitute forms of schooling that are more individualized or centered around students, even if it gets good press and finds some kind of market, seems destined eventually to fail.

Many of the teacher-powered schools use competencies as the basis of evaluating learning, and this approach completely avoids the time-locked pace that characterizes most traditional classroom practices.

And some schools have in recent times distinguished themselves for departing from the long-held model. Summit Schools, for example, now numbering about 400, have elected to be different and have not failed. Most schools in the charter management organization's portfolio rely on project-learning, emphasize personalization with students, build in substantial self-reliance among students and tend to be teacher-led operations. Most such schools, like Summit, are in the chartered sector of public schooling. And they still have age-grading.

Back in 1910, Thomas Edison, then regarded as the most prolific inventor of both ideas and innovations, once demonstrated his talking picture machines to a crowd of school principals. According to the Edmund Morris biography, the principals regarded his technology "as a threat to their trusted old ways of teaching."

Edison, brilliant but naïve about the system he faced, thought that using new media "to explore astronomy, bacteriology, physics, forestry, fine art, and zoology would bring the joy back to education."

Fast forward to the hallmark 1983 U.S. report *A Nation at Risk*, the product of President Ronald Reagan's National Commission on Excellence in Education, said there was "a rising tide of mediocrity." It put education on the national stage, with international tables showing how far behind the United States was falling. Governors convened in 1989 in Charlottesville, Virginia, and buffeted by the reports references to declines in student achievement, adopted a set of goals for America. The United States would be first in this and that by a date certain. No goal was ever achieved.

The 1990s brought the period of standards-based reform. But standards evolved into standardization. The idea that making everything the same would be better was prevailing. Reading and math got most of the attention. Subjects like art and music disappeared from many schools. In recent years, Marshall Smith, who along with Jennifer O'Day, wrote the paper that people recognize as setting off the standards movement, has conceded that standards did not work, did not make a dent in the performance of American students.

In the early 2000s, the NCLB law, while inaugurating a period of blaming teachers for poor results, did unmask the uneven results of the system the nation had built. This law, and its requirements to report achievement by race, made it quite evident that there were large gaps. Today, in many states, the achievement gap has become a kind of meme. The gap in academic performance between whites and students of color is the cloud that defines the sky.

As whites (and often Asians) have done better in the system, the statistical achievement gap grows. And perhaps the United States does better with what we have long called "minorities," but that gap persists and shows up every time achievement is displayed or discussed.

Educators who go regularly to regional and national conferences are now accustomed to the nearly ritualistic lamentations about the achievement gap. The issue is prominent in so many conferences. And always, there are promises to do anything, everything that it takes to close the gap.

The truth about the achievement gap is starkly simple. The gap, as it is conventionally defined, is permanent and likely to grow wider until and unless educators get serious about making schools student-centered. And get serious about what achievement means to individual students. That is the truth that it seems few are willing to admit or discuss.

EE focuses much of its organizational energy on making schooling more student-centered. As a result, as an organization, it has done more to explain and illustrate exactly what this often used term actually means. EE's student-centered graph is worth anyone's study, shown below as Figure 7.1.

Converting "achievement " to "opportunity"—is that better language or just a dodge, as some people claim? The terms used become irrelevant if the school is designed to offer personalized learning. There still may be unequal outcomes, but everyone is closer to their own potential. That is a good feeling—one that most students never thought they would have.

Christina Samuels, writing for *Education Week* in early 2020, reported on the periodical's recent survey of teachers about the achievement gap. As she wrote, 75 percent of teachers said that student performance was most affected by factors outside of school. "It's not our fault," as she put it. Only "student motivation" made the top tier of results and "school quality" showed up in the next tier. What Samuels did not say, but many teachers might, is you are not at fault when you have almost no control over what matters in school. You have systems in place over which teachers have little influence.

She did point out that, according to EdBuild, a nonprofit working on school finance issues, "minority districts get $23 billion less in funding nationally than majority-white districts."

Some states, however, whether through differences in property taxes or other fiscal variations, allocate more to their urban schools which disproportionately enroll minority students. So, national averages must be explained. But even schools with more funding have gaps, so while money matters, it is not the whole story.

Some observers point out, rightly so, that having more teachers of color would positively affect this gap. But Black or Latinx teachers are in short supply, just to name two categories. Some claim, with justification, that teachers of color are not so much in short supply as they are just good judges of what is a decent job or career; many of them have concluded it is not. Those who emerge from colleges of education are only in single-digit percentages and are snapped up immediately.

Conclusion

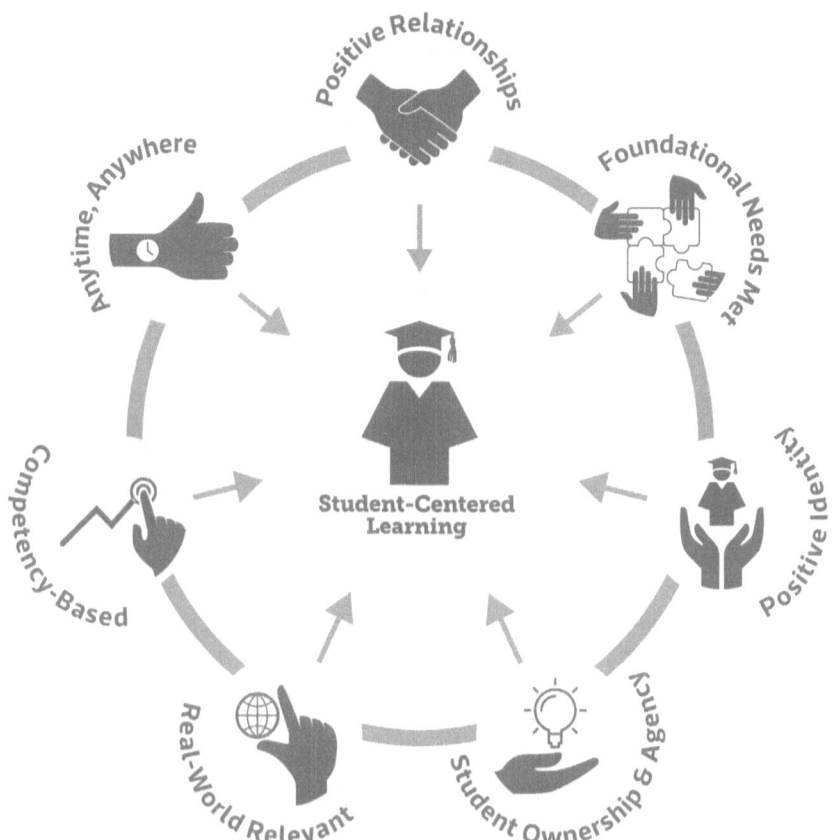

Figure 7.1 EE Student-Centered Principles. *Education Evolving.*

And even though race is not a factor in reductions, teachers of color, likely the newest teachers, tend to be the first to be cut, when last-in, first-out policies are used. And they quit at higher rates. According to Ingersoll's work, those quitting list a lack of administrative support, tying compensation to student results, lack of classroom autonomy, poor teaching conditions, and other career interests as reasons to leave.

The former mayor of New Orleans and now CEO of the National Urban League, Marc Morial, has picked up on the organization's longstanding commitment to greater equity for minority students. He told Jim Cowen, writing for *Education Week*, that "equity will be achieved when our education system provides each and every student with the necessary resources to reach their full potential and to be ready for college and life."

The system simply cannot deliver what the public expects—for all students. The public needs to make the new deal with teachers.

Chapter 7
THE WHOLE SYSTEM DOES NOT HAVE TO CHANGE

There is an assumption that often goes unchallenged: that to make a change in a large system, that everything has to change, all at once. That nearly never happens. And for the teacher-powered movement to become a consequential force in American education, all it needs is an open door, permission to try things, space to demonstrate that teachers know how to get results in a school.

But the change-everything idea remains the assumption. The latest example may be the state of Maryland's sweeping blueprint for schooling all over the state. When the Commission on Innovation and Excellence in Education reported its findings, the Speaker of the House in Maryland called them "devastating." Governor Larry Hogan vetoed the bill for funding as the session ended. The effort to make the system work better persists.

The chair of the commission, former chancellor of the Maryland's university system, called for an oversight board to monitor better student performance, and, in particular, a better record for attracting and retaining good teachers. Nothing about changing the system. Just exhortation to make it work better.

As Christensen said so often, those in a large system who are expected to deliver something different have to have separate organizational space in which to work. IBM could not have produced a personal computer without sending those engineers to a Boca Raton warehouse and giving them the autonomy to just build a good personal computer. Providing that separate space enabled IBM to become the only computing company that survived the disruption that rocked the industry.

How Target was launched is not only a good story but a ready example of the necessity of giving something new separate space. Bruce Dayton, one of the five brothers who had taken over the reins of the Dayton's department stores, which later became Dayton-Hudson, was interviewed by a small EE team only a couple of years before he died. He recalled meetings with his brothers in the early 1960s. "We knew," he said, "that the department store was a dying breed of cat." Not an elegant analogy, perhaps, but to the point. Indeed, the brothers' conferences took place as discount retailing was getting underway, and Sam Walton was about to launch what became WalMart. And Kresge was starting to operate K-marts. Why, the Dayton brothers asked themselves, would people need to come to any downtown to a comprehensively merchandised department store?

The Dayton brothers knew the answer. So they launched a new store, at first in Roseville, Minnesota, in 1962, calling it Target. The key business decision, as Dayton told the group, was to have the stores report directly to the CEO and the board, not to the department store.

Conclusion

Though this was long before Clayton Christensen made the theory of disruptive innovation famous in business circles, they were making the right disruptive decision. In effect, they were saying to Target managers: do as well as you can, get as big as you might, and if you take over the whole company, that's OK. Which is what happened.

That is exactly what the system should do with the teacher-powered movement. Will it happen? So far, it is happening in the chartered sector, where there is more freedom to be different. And notably in some districts, though the path to sustainability is not easy.

Teachers are trapped in the system. As Michael Horn, one of the authors of *Disrupting Class* put it, "People are not stupid even though they may look like they are doing dumb things. They probably work in a dumb organization. People react to the culture they are in." That is the system. We cannot change it. But it is possible to get permission to be different. That is all that lawmakers should do. That is all that is needed.

How bad does it have to get for some places to change. Massive numbers are hitting the streets and staying for weeks because a police shooting in Minneapolis ignited fury that was building. Sundin, that tireless warhorse who broke so many rules in her time as head of the Minneapolis Federation of Teachers and activist leader of TURN, probably said it best: "We have all railed against the industrial model of education that still conforms to an ancient agrarian calendar and school days based on bus schedules and classes based on chronological age."

Brookins, who can point to a higher percentage of board-certified teachers from teacher-powered schools than in other schools, thinks "there are thousands of teachers who are interested in more professionalism." She's right. But there has to be separate space and a new deal.

Graba, cited several times in this book, has a way of reducing something complex to a simple sentence. Here is his take on the dilemma: "Everybody wants school to be better, but almost nobody wants it to be different."

To become what it should be, the teacher-powered movement is ready to accept the new deal: all the accountability the public expects for the authority over student and school success.

Epilogue

As the manuscript for this book was being reviewed, a pandemic began sweeping the world. People gradually absorbed the implications. It was almost a prelapsarian moment, a newfound innocence. It commenced a period of profound perplexity for most people.

Many people started using masks and discovered physical distancing and how to avoid social congregating. It still does not seem natural, but the population generally went along with these measures.

The spring of 2020 saw a rash of prognostications about how different things will be at the end of the pandemic. Some predict the end of globalization—with its supply chains and trading practices—along with a continued reluctance to get on planes, or cruise ships, show up for concerts, or take kids to crowded amusement parks.

Most likely, that is a list of reflexive, and wrong, notions. But some things will surely be different. The pandemic's sweeping impact will accelerate some trends already under way, such as the trends in retail. It may change work habits, possibly land use. The disease certainly exposed weaknesses in preparation at all levels and in all sectors. Schools that had not adapted to technological change were slow to react, reluctant to shift to remote modes, and have not so far done well with school changes.

Zaynab Baalbaki, a teacher at the Escuela Verde on the southside of Milwaukee and a teacher-powered schools ambassador, told a webinar audience in June of 2020 how it could be different. Her school believes what EE teaches with student-centered learning principles, embodying particularly the one about positive relationships. She described how her school rapidly built on the platforms it already had, relying on Google Classroom, providing hotspots for kids with little or no access to the Internet, distributing the laptops they had from school to kids directly. She said the school was able to capitalize on the flexibility teachers had to make it easier for students. She reached out to them with texts to be sure they were connected. This pattern is typical of teacher-powered schools.

Another teacher, Jake Fields, the lead teacher at Wildlands School near Eau Claire, Wisconsin, told the webinar audience that when the pandemic arrived in force, it felt like a "day-wrecker" does when rock suddenly collides with the bottom of your canoe. But, as he went on to say, the most important thing to get right in a crisis is putting "relationships first, " just like what Baalbaki's school had done. That is what matters. If you do not get this fundamental right, nothing else will work. Fields pointed out that, properly structured, kids could have an experience on Zoom, which is a lot like sitting around a lunch table. And he was always looking for the "silver lining," as he put it, what we could learn from this situation that we always needed to know.

But if students of history confine the scope to just schooling, some things have certainly been exposed. The same kids who were at the wrong end of the achievement gap still were; turns out many of them lacked devices or certainly good access to the internet. Not all schools made devices immediately available or added hotspots to ensure steady access to the Internet.

And as distance became the norm, it was painfully obvious that students with special needs require some contact with professionals. This situation will continue to be a challenge.

And many kids who always disliked school still did. Teachers reported some students proved elusive once the drill shifted to an online world. Now they could avoid school altogether. Why did society put up with this situation so long? If kids disliked school, what were the reasons? If they quit, schools need to understand why they are leaving.

Is it just possible that staying at home more began to break through the deeply embedded hurdle of thinking "real school" is a place, a building in a district with multiple schools, commanded by a board and superintendent, where teachers essentially do as they are told?

And is the pandemic raising the chances that teachers unions might see real possibilities of a different future, one in which they support the aspirations of some willing teachers to take charge of what matters in schools?

Will foundations—not only the huge Bill and Melinda Gates Foundation but the thousands of smaller ones—begin to support groups of teachers who are willing and ready to take charge of what matters for student and school success?

Will state legislatures, clearly the macro boards for all public schools in the United States, put grant money on the line and loosen the regulatory apron wrapped around schools? Will they enable groups of teachers to take on full responsibility for schools?

Most of all, will parents and the public imagine what is possible with a new blend of what teachers do best with what technology makes possible? Some teachers have discovered a new and better way of connecting with students—and with some with whom connections were always elusive if not completely impossible. Kids with special needs, and those who just were too shy to be very open in a full classroom, suddenly became real individuals during this crisis. That surprised some teachers.

But mostly, if written accounts may be believed, schools tried to replicate what was happening in classrooms. And in these cases, kids found what they had to do was boring at best. Zoom may not have been well known, but all kinds of other apps and software for getting online were second nature to many students. But replicating the classroom was a dud and an embarrassment to the system. Software that is good, effective, and continually vetted has been available for over a decade. It gets better all the time. Sure, profiteers caused some reputational damage, but the technology available has been growing in quality and effectiveness for a long time.

In John Lienhard's "How Invention Begins," he jars readers' memories by citing the introduction of distance learning long ago—but "now to be delivered by the Internet rather than the postman." He was way ahead of his time, talking from the 1940s. When Lienhard, still in high school in 1946, was given a correspondence course on drafting, he recalled that "the world opened up, for now no instructor was talking at me and obstructing my view of the subject. I was on my own and education made sense." The International Correspondence School soon had a quarter million students. That was long ago.

Fast forward to 2020 and Sal Khan, who founded Khan Academy in 2004 from the epiphany he had helping his niece, then twelve years old (she is now twenty-eight), conquer basic math problems. When Khan hears people fret over screen time, he reminds that all screen time is not equal. He advises teachers and parents to first find out what drives kids' interests and then simply pick two or three pieces of software.

Has the virus situation exposed what many knew all along—that some kids did not have good connections to the world via the Internet at home? That they relied on what they got in school (often for basic nutrition too)? Of course. But that is a problem that can be solved, with a lot less money than has been spent coping with the pandemic.

Three school districts did spend the money and they were not all markedly affluent places. They took the time and spent the money to get all teachers ready for what technology could do for both connections to students and academic gains, long before the pandemic hit. For these districts, getting into technology seemed necessary, not really optional. According to a recent Edutopia blog, the Lindsey Unified School District in the central valley of

California knew that they were serving farm families and that kids often had to do their school work independently.

Further south in California, another district, the Cajon Valley Union District, could not afford adding anything without a special bond election, but it passed and they invested in technology. And all the way across the country, the much larger Miami-Dade County Public Schools years ago plumped for bonding to finance everything from devices for every student to beefing up Wi-Fi all over. To them, it was all about equity. For many, perhaps most districts in the United States, the pandemic exposed obvious equity issues among students. Too many lacked devices and likely access to reliable Wi-Fi.

So, when the pandemic came and schools began to close, these three districts were ready. They already had a blended curriculum with good lists from which students could pick and choose. Surely there are more.

Why lament the unavailability and unaffordability of a chemistry class in a remote rural school when software has long been available that is better than most chemistry classes? The same goes for languages and the arts or even economics (still not often offered). And who is better at explaining math than the videos produced by Khan Academy? Where is there a better platform for learning than the likes of Google Classroom or even the games of Web-based Kahoot? Some may be best right now, but there is serious competition in this field and that not only produces more vendors but usually continuously improves quality.

There are plenty of critics of online learning and defenders of the belief in what constitutes real school. In a blog for The 74, Robert Pondiscio argued that there is no new normal, that kids will go back to regular school soon. He seems to think, at least at the time he wrote, that the pandemic is only an emergency situation. That real school is a cultural habit the nation would not break.

Even the esteemed *Economist* magazine, in a spring 2020 editorial says that "virtual school is less good than the real thing." "Let the children in, let them learn," the editorial goes on to implore. Many others predict lower achievement by all students as a consequence of schools being closed, with lifelong harm and widened inequality.

State officials, all over, lamented that it had become difficult to "deliver instruction," terminology apparently not subject to the virus.

Some understand though that not only is change inevitable, but it may be good. The Organization for Economic and Community Development's (OECD) Andreas Schleicher, who oversees the Programme for International Student Assessment (PISA) for seventy-nine nations, says that nearly half of today's students cite job aspirations that are clearly 19th- or 20th-century jobs; they likely won't exist in many numbers when these kids burst onto the job market. "If we limit our children's' experience to just what happens in the classroom," he points out, "then it's going to make it a lot harder for them to see where they fit in the world."

Governors such as Andrew Cuomo of New York, who rose to unprecedented prominence in his management of the virus situation in his state, calls for a "smarter system of education."

Some may be listening. The school district in Cleveland, Ohio, may boast of a multitude of experiments and many experiences. But the district CEO, Eric Gordon, told Patrick O'Donnell of The 74 newsletter that the district will welcome its students back after the pandemic pause, but *not* to the old age-graded system. Instead, the district is shifting to "multi-age bands" that allow students to work toward mastery at their own speed, with emphasis on the high school level. Gordon is the current chair of the Council of Great City Schools and told the reporter that other big city heads were calling him, saying they were looking at doing something similar.

Skepticism is warranted, though, not the least because the union in Cleveland has not signed off on the shift. But the pandemic has opened a new door. Is a complete operating system shift likely? No, according to Christensen's thinking, because the systems' values eventually stipulate other priorities. Their processes compel them to do things a different way. And the mindset of most parents, lawmakers, and voters is deeply embedded in conventional notions of what real school is.

Jackie Bennett, who may be mostly concerned about the PROSE schools in New York city, worries generally about what schools will do next year, if the pandemic is still on. "Can we just create the physical distances and tell kids to come half a day, so we can accommodate all of them," she wonders. Well, if districts remain as compliance-oriented as most are today, the answer is yes. And even the PROSE school people, accustomed as they are to breaking rules, have to live with the city's central notions about real school. But PROSE teachers may be the vanguard of a different breed of teacher, able and willing to show a better way even if the prevailing guidance is to be like other schools. Schools where teachers have significant influence just seem substantially different from other schools. We may soon find out whether that leads to real change.

Some, like the author David Osborne, draw on more hope from seeing how the Indianapolis area has used the Innovation Zone concept to develop better schools, to break old molds, to defy expectations. Maybe this independent approach, even with the old ideas about what makes a school real, will get there. Will teachers there rise up, take responsibility, be different?

Osborne also sees considerable hope too in the new systems of schools in New Orleans that formed in the wake of the disastrous hurricane Katrina in

2005. Most of the schools are chartered which bolsters Osborne's confidence, though it is widely admitted that the forces that benefited from the old system (including the teachers' union) are still present.

Something similar to Indianapolis is happening in Springfield, Massachusetts, as one isolated example. Massachusetts is a state with authority for takeover of poor schools and Springfield had a bunch. But as Osborne reports, instead of a conventional state takeover, Chris Gabrieli of Boston organized a nonprofit organization that took on 10 schools, with a board that blends governance from the district, the state, and the city. Gabrieli is the chair. In this case, the local union bought in (though the state union is decidedly against the model spreading).

Again, the key was nurturing the notion of an Innovation Zone, with the nonprofit acting, as Osborne puts it, "almost as an authorizer, as you would in the charter sector." And these schools, which consistently produced results (using the metrics that still matter most) that were not up to par, are doing significantly better. Is it the Innovation Zone distinction? Is it the nonprofit board delivering closer attention and bringing more resources?

No matter what the answers are for schools in an Innovation Zone, the general conclusion is no longer mysterious: teachers are the ultimate catalysts for that better system, if there is to be one that spreads and lasts. As this book has claimed over and over, once teachers are in charge, they feel fully accountable. And once they see the wide range of proficiencies among students, they know they have to personalize the learning experience. Education has to be student-centered. Perhaps the only way America will ever make education effective and equitable is the turn schools over to teachers. Only teachers are likely to make education student-centered. They will because they want every kid to succeed, to reach whatever potential each one has. And they will because they have to.

There was never a better time than now to suggest turning schools over to teachers. Unless giving teachers real authority over their work is just too obvious.

Bibliography

Archer, Jeff. President Leaves Mixed Record on Pledge to 'Reinvent' NEA. *Education Week*, June 19, 2002.

Auletta, Ken. *Googled: The End of the World As We Know It*. New York: Penguin Books, 2015.

Baubach Eugene, and Eric Patashnik. *A Practical Guide to Policy Analysis*. Thousand Oaks, CA: Sage Publishing, 2020.

Brown, Tim. *Change by Design: How Design Thinking Transforms Organizations and Inspires Innovation*. New York: HarperCollins, 2009.

Burnett, Daarel II. Face It. School Governance Is a Mess. *Education Week*, January 20, 2020.

Bryk, Anthony, Gomez, Louis, Grunow, Alicia, and LeMahieu, Paul. *Learning to Improve*. Cambridge: Harvard University Press, 2015.

Carr, Sarah. Where Teachers Rule: A School with No Principal? *Milwaukee Journal-Sentinel*, June 11, 2005, Section B.

Center for Education and the Workforce, Georgetown University. ROI of Liberal Arts Colleges. Washington, DC: Washington Post, January 13, 2020.

Childress, Herbert. Seventeen Reasons Why Football is Better Than High School. *Phi Delta Kappan International*, 4(8), 616–619, 1998.

Christensen, Clayton M. *The Innovator's Dilemma*. Cambridge MA: Harvard Business School Press, 1997.

Christensen, Clayton M., Horn, Michael, and Johnson, Curtis W. *Disrupting Class: How disruptive Innovation will change the way the World Learns*. New York: McGraw-Hill, 2008.

Christensen, Clayton M., and Overdorf, Michael. Meeting the Challenge of Disruptive Change, *Harvard Business Review*, 78(2), 66–77, 2000.

Chubb, J.E., and Moe, T.M. *Politics Markets and America's Schools*. Washington, DC: The Brookings Institution, 1990.

Cuban, L. Blog: *Please Don't Hype Teacher-Run Schools*, 2010.

Cuban, L. Blog: *Challenging the Grammar of Schooling* (Part 3). 2019.

Dirkswager, ed. (editor) *Teachers As Owners.* Lanham, MD: Scarecrow Press of Rowman and Littlefield Education, 2002.
Eels, Rachel J. *A Meta-Analysis of the Relationship of Collective Teacher Efficacy and Student Achievement.* A Loyola University of Chicago dissertation, 2011.
Farris-Berg, K., and Dirkswager, E. *Trusting Teachers with School Success: What happens when teachers call the shots.* Lanham, MD: Rowman and Littlefield Education, 2013.
Ferlazzo, Larry. We Might Have Got Remote Learning Wrong. *Education Week,* 2020.
Gladwell, Malcolm. *The Tipping Point: How Little Things Can Make a Big Difference.* Boston: Little, Brown, 2002.
Goddard, Roger, Goodard, Y., Hoy, W., and Hoy, A. Collective Teacher Efficacy: its Meaning, Measure and Impact on Student Achievement. *American Education Research Journal,* 37(2), 479–507, 2000.
Goddard, Roger, Hoy W., and Hoy, A. Collective Teacher Efficacy: Theoretical Developments, Empirical Evidence, and Future Directions. *Educational Researcher,* 33(3), 3–13, 2004.
Goddard, Roger, Skria, Linda, and Solloum, Serena. The Role of Collective Efficacy in Closing Achievement Gaps: a Mixed Methods Study of School Leadership for Excellence and Equity. *Journal of Education for Students Placed at Risk,* 22(4), 220–236, 2017.
Gosner, Sarah. *How Long Term Tech Planning Pays Off – Now and In the Future.* A blog of Edutopia, May 4, 2020.
Haigler, A., and Owens, B. *Open Up Education – How Open Way Learning Can Transform Schools.* Lanham, MD: Rowman & Littlefield, 2018.
Hamilton, Laura, Stecher, Brian, and Kun Yuan. *Standards-Based Reform in the United States: History, Research, and Future Directions.* RAND Corporation, 2008.
Hawkins, B. Teacher Cooperatives: What Happens When Teachers Run the School. *Education Next,* 9, 37–41, 2001.
Hess, F.M. *The Cage-Busting Teacher.* Cambridge, MA: Harvard University Press, 2015.
Hess, F.M., and Manno, B. *Customized Schooling: Beyond Whole School Reform.* Cambridge, MA: Harvard University Press, 2011.
Hill, Paul. *What New Orleans Can Teach Us About the Forces Blocking Change in Education.* Seattle: Center for Reinventing Public Education, The Lens, February 6, 2020.
Hirschman. A.O. *Exit, Voice and Loyalty: Response to Decline in Firms, Organizations, and States.* Cambridge, MA: Harvard University Press, 1970.
Ingersoll, Richard M. *Who Controls Teachers Work: Power and Accountability in America's schools.* Cambridge, MA: Harvard University Press, 2003.
Ingersoll, Richard, Sirinides, Philip, and Dougherty, Patrick. *Leadership Matters.* American Educator, Spring 2018, 13–17. Washington, DC: American Federation of Teachers.
Ingersoll, Richard M., Sirinides, Philip and Dougherty, Patrick. *School Leadership: Teachers' Role in Decision making and Student Achievement.* Consortium for

Policy Research in Education. Latham, MD: Rowman and Littlefield Education, 2017.

Issacson, Walter. *Steve Jobs.* New York: Simon and Schuster, 2011.

Johnson, Susan Moore. *Finders and Keepers*: *Helping New Teachers Survive and Thrive in Our Schools.* San Francisco, CA: Jossey-Bass, 2004.

Kemper, Sara. An unpublished University of Minnesota dissertation featuring field work of teacher-powered schools, 2020.

Kennedy, Paul. *Engineers of Victory: The Problem Solvers Who Turned the Tide in the Second World War.* New York: Random House, 2013.

Kerchner, Charles, Koppich, Julia, and Weeres, Joseph. *United Mind Workers: Unions and Teaching in the Knowledge Society.* San Francisco, CA: Jossey-Bass, 1997

Kerchner, Charles, Koppich, Julia, and Weeres, Joseph. *Taking Charge of Quality: How Teachers and Unions Can Revitalize Schools.* San Francisco, CA: Jossey-Bass, 1998.

Kolderie, Ted. *Improvement + Innovation.* Edina, MN: Beavers Pond Press, 2014.

Kolderie, Ted. *The Split Screen Strategy: How to Turn Education into a Self-Improving System.* Edina, MN: Beavers Pond Press, 2015.

Kolderie, Ted. *Thinking Out the How.* Edina, MN: Beavers Pond Press, 2018.

Kuhn, Thomas. *The Structure of Scientific Revolutions.* Chicago, IL: University of Chicago Press, 1970.

Langhorne, Emily. An Unlikely Alliance: Here's What Can Happen if Teachers Unions Embrace Charter Schools. *Forbes Magazine*, September 11, 2018.

Lienhard, John H. *How Invention Begins: Echoes of Old Voices in the Rise of New Machines.* New York: Oxford University Press, 2006.

Lipsky, Martin. *Street Level Bureaucracy: Dilemmas of the Individual in Public Services.* New York: Russell Sage Foundation, 1980,

Lytle, James H. *Working for Kids.* Lanham, MD. Rowman & Littlefield Education, 2010.

Lytle, James H. Prospects for Reforming. *Urban Education*, 27(2), 109–131, 1992.

McDonald, Tim. *Unsustainable: A Strategy for Making Public Schooling More Productive, Effective and Affordable.* Lanham, MD: Rowman and Littlefield, 2011.

Merrow, John. *The Influence of Teachers*: *Reflections on Teaching and Leadership.* New York: L.M. Books, 2011.

Metz, Mary. *Real School – a Universal Drama and Disparate Experience.* Educational Politics for the New Century, 25–91. New York: Falmer Press, 1990.

Moe, Terry. *Special Interests*: *Teachers Unions and America's Public Schools.* Washington, DC: Brookings Institution Press, 2011.

Moe, Terry. *The Politics of Institutional Reform: Katrina, Education and the Second Face of Power.* Cambridge: Cambridge University Press, 2019.

Nathan, Joe. *Free to Teach: Achieving Equity and Excellence in Schools.* Cleveland, OH: Pilgrim Press, 1983.

O'Donnell, Patrick. Cleveland Schools Considering Bold Plan to Confront Virus Learning Loss: A 'Mastery' Learning Initiative That Would Scrap Grade Levels, Let Kids Learn at Own Pace. *The 74 Newsletter*, May 20, 2020.

Osborne, David. *Reinventing America's Schools: Creating a Twenty-first Century Education System.* New York: Bloomberg USA, 2017.

Ouchi, William G. *Making Schools Work: a Revolutionary Plan to Get Your Children the Education They Need.* New York: Simon and Schuster, 2003.

Pink, Daniel. *Drive: The Surprising Truth About What Motivates Us.* New York: Riverhead Books, 2009.

Reichgott-Junge, Ember. *Zero Change of Passage: The Pioneering Charter School Story.* Edina, MN: Beavers Pond Press, 2012.

Rogers, Everett. *The Diffusion of Innovations*, 5th edition. New York: Free Press, 2003.

Samuels, Christina. Who's to Blame for the Black-White Achievement Gap? *Education Week*, January 7, 2020.

Shindler, John. *Transformative Classroom Management.* San Francisco, CA: Jossey-Bass, 2009.

Smith, Marshall S., and O'Day, Jennifer. Systemic School Reform. *Journal of Education Policy*, 5(5), 233–267, 1990.

Stoll, John D. Can Design Thinking Save Business? *Wall Street Journal*, January 31, 2020.

Toch, Thomas. *In the Name of Excellence: The Struggle to Reform the Nation's Schools and What Should Be Done?* New York: Oxford University Press, 1991.

Tweed, P., and Seubert, L. *An Improbable School: Transforming How Teachers Teach and Students Learn.* Lead the Path LLC, 2015.

Tyack, David. *The One Best System.* Cambridge, MA: Harvard University Press, 1974.

Tyack, David, and Cuban, Larry. *Tinkering with Utopia: a Century of Public School Reform.* Cambridge, MA: Harvard University Press, 1997.

Wagner, Tony. *The Global Achievement Gap: Why Even our Best Schools Don't Teach the New Survival Skills our Students Need and What We Can Do About It.* Cambridge, MA: Harvard University Press, 2008.

Wagner, Tony. *Creating Innovators: The Making of Young People Who Will Change the World.* New York: Scribner, 2012.

Winkler, Elizabeth. Laszlo Bock Thinks Machine Learning Can Make Work Better? *Wall Street Journal*, January 31, 2020.

Wise, A. E. Toward Equality of Educational Opportunity: What's Most Promising? *Phi Delta Kappan Journal*, 100(8), 8–13, 2019.

OTHER SOURCES

Excerpts from Texas Education magazine. Winter 2019-20 edition.

Interview with Albert Shanker, *United Against a Common Foe.* America's Agenda, Spring, 1992.

Interview with Bruce Dayton, at The Marsh, Minnetonka, Minnesota, September 21, 2007.

Interview with Ted Sanders, 2009, with Joe Graba of Education Evolving, in Denver, Colorado.
Interview with Larry Rosenstock, founder of High Tech High, in San Diego, California, January, 2017, with Brad Blue.
Notes from board meetings of Charter Friends Network, 1990s.
Notes from minutes of board meetings of National Charter School Alliance, early 2000s.
Notes of observer at Mackinac Island meeting of organizers of National Alliance for Public Charter Schools, 2005.
Notes from Curtis Johnson visit to Urban Assembly for Green Careers school, 2019.
Notes of Ted Kolderie on Site Management in Edmonton, Canada, 1990.
Notes of Curtis Johnson from webinar of ChangeED, June, 2020.
Notes of Ted Kolderie on discussions about Teacher Ownership and Teacher Unions from the TURN meeting, February 7, 2003.
Notes from Curtis Johnson visit to policy conference at the School of Public Affairs, University of Colorado at Denver, 2019.
Phi Delta Kappan - polls in 2008 and 2019.
Speech of Charles Kerchner to the National Education Association Pacific Region Summit, 2009. ("Things That Go Bump in the Night.")

Index

Note: Page references for figures are italicized.

Academia del Lenguaje y Bellas Artes (ALBA), 20
accountability: for charter schools, 58; in coaching athletics, 13; resistance to, 13; in teacher-powered schools, 7, 26, 68; without authority, 9–10
achievement gap, 71–72, 78
administrators, 6–7, 9, 10, 11
age-grading, xxiii, 69, 70, 71, 81
American Federation of Teachers (AFT), 61, 67
Andrekopolous, Bill, 2, 19–20
Andres, Bill, xxi
Auletta, Ken, 54
authority, teacher. *See* autonomy
autonomies, critical, xxv, 28, 29, *30*, 44
autonomy (authority): in coaching athletics, 13; culture shift toward, xxiv; defined, xxv; examples of, 18–23; mindset objections to, 13–14, 23; pandemic adaptation and, 81; positive results of, *33*, 33–34; public perspectives on, *38*; student performance and, 14, 31–34, 72; student responsibility and, 13, 14; teacher interest in, 4; in teacher-powered schools, xxi, 14–15, 16, 26, 68; teacher retention and, 34–36, 64, 73; teacher satisfaction and, 19, *33*, *33*, 34; teacher unions and, 63–65, 67–68; in traditional schools, 9–10, 16–17, 66
Avalon School, 39

Baalbaki, Zaynab, 77–78
Bacal, Lincoln, 13, 66
Bakken, Carrie, 38–39
Bennett, Jackie, 21, 81
Berg, Erik, 21, 59
Blaine amendments, 65
Boasberg, Tom, 15
Bobb, Robert, 9
Boston pilot schools, 20–21
Boston Teachers Union (BTU), 21
Brookins, Peggy, 65, 75
Brooks, Herb, 13
Bryk, Tony, 58
Burnett, Daarel II, 56
burn-out, teacher, 7, 34, 47
Bush Foundation, 50

Cajon Valley Union District, 80
Carnegie Foundation for the Advancement of Teaching, xxiii

Carnegie Unit, 70
Casap, Jaime, xxiv
Center for Collaborative Education, 20, 56–57
Center for Reinventing Public Education, 56
Center for Teacher Quality (CTQ), 28, 41, 43
change: acceleration of, 66; drivers of, 43, 65; incremental *vs.* radical, 74; in public school systems, 54–56, 64–67, 80–81; resistance to, 18, 36, 38, 50, 56, 69; S-curves for, 54, 55; technology and, 36, 65–66
Charter Management Organizations (CMOs), 58
charter schools: emergence and evolution of, 57–59; innovation in, 71, 75; Innovation Schools law and, 15–16; parent involvement in, 43; *vs.* pilot schools, 16; private education and, 54; teacher education and, 49; *vs.* teacher-powered schools, 58; union opposition to, 67
Charter Schools Growth Fund, 58
Chase, Bob, 62
Childress, Herb, 13
Christensen, Clayton, xv, 50, 74, 75, 81. *See also Disrupting Class*
Chubb, John, 61
CMOs. *See* Charter Management Organizations (CMOs)
collaboration, 7, 12, 51
collective teacher efficacy, 32
Columbia University Klingenstein Center, 51
Commission on Innovation and Excellence in Education, 74
competencies, evaluating learning with, 71
Cortina, Walter, 23
Council of Great City Schools, 11
Cowen, Jim, 73
Coyne, Frank, 15–16
credit, units of, 70

CTQ. *See* Center for Teacher Quality (CTQ)
Cuban, Larry, xxiv, 69, 70
culture of encouragement, 12–13
Cuomo, Andrew, 81
Customized Schooling (Hess, Manno), 51–52

Dalton Plan, xxiii
Dayton, Bruce, 74
Deasy, John, 16
Decker, Kerry, 22
Detroit Public Schools, 9
Dirkswager, Ed, xxvi, 25, 26, 28
Disraeli, Benjamin, 68
Disrupting Class (Christensen, Horn, et al.), 36, 54
distance learning, 79. *See also* online education
Donnelly, Josef, 37–38
Drinan, Betsy, 21
Duncan, Arne, 38–40

Eastman, George, 12
EdBuild, 72
Edison, Thomas, 71
Edmonton public schools, 18–19
Education Evolving (EE) network: critical autonomies used by, xxv, 29, 44; in development of teacher-powered schools, 28–29; movement growth and, 53; publicity push, 41, 42, 43; student-centered focus of, 72, *73*; teacher-powered schools supported by, xiv, 4; teacher survey, xxv, 4, 30–31
Education Week, 56
Eels, Rachel Jean, 32
Eight Year Study, xxiii
Engineers of Victory (Kennedy), 12
Enloe, Walter, 49
equity, 32, 37, 73, 80
Esdal, Lars, 58–59
Every Student Succeeds Act (ESSA, 2015), 10

Farris-Berg, Kim, xxvi, 25, 26, 28
Fields, Jake, 78
focused instruction, 11
French, Dan, 20, 57
Frymier, Jack, xxii, xxiii
Fuller, Howard, 58
funding, xxvi, 47, 65, 72

Gabrieli, Chris, 82
The Global Achievement Gap (Wagner), 49
Goddard, Roger, 32
Goddard, Yvonne, 32
Goodyear, Charles, 12
Gordon, Eric, 81
Graba, Joe, xxvii, 10–11, 20, 38–39, 68, 75
Green School (Denver), 15
Green School (New York City), 8, 22
Groff, Peter, 15
the Guild, 67

Hagberg, Erika, xxiv
Haugen, Jay, 13–14
Hedy, John, xiv
Hess, Rick, 51–52
High School in the Community, 26
High Tech High Graduate School of Education, 49, 50, 51, 59
Hill, Paul, 56
Hogan, Larry, 74
Horn, Michael, xv, 75. *See also Disrupting Class*
"How Invention Begins" (Lienhard), 79
Hoy, Anita, 32
Hoy, Wayne, 32
Hunter College, New York City, NY, 51
Hurricane Katrina, 70, 81–82

IBM, 74
Individualized Developmental Educational Approaches to Learning (IDEAL), Milwaukee, WI, 2–3, 19–20

Ingersoll, Richard: mindset objection encountered by, 14, 23; on teacher autonomy, xiv, 26, 33–34; on teacher retention, 35–36, 73; on teacher voice, 44–45
Innovation Schools law, 15–16
Innovation Zone, Indianapolis, 81, 82
International Community School, 37–38
International Correspondence School, 79

Jobs, Steve, 11
Johnson, Susan Moore, 37
Johnson, Verne, xxi
Junge, Amy: on governance support, 46; grant-writing and planning support, 45; on high-performing organizations, 25; on movement growth, 59; resistance expected by, 16; school qualifications influenced by, 28, 44; on teacher motivation, 36–37; on variation among teacher-powered schools, 29
Junge, Ember Reichgott, 58

Kahlenberg, Richard, 59
Kemper, Sara, 33, 34
Kennedy, Paul, 12
Kerchner, Charles, 55, 59–60
Khan, Sal, 56, 79
Kodak, 55
Kolderie, Ted: advocacy efforts, 38–39; on charter school evolution, 57, 58; on clarifications needed for growth, 54; Graba and, 10–11; on origins of teacher-powered schools movement, 26; perspective of, xiv–xv

Langhorne, Emily, 16
Learning from L.A. (Kerchner), 55
Learning to Improve (Byrk), 58
Levine, Arthur, 49
liberal arts education, xxiv
Lienhard, John, 79
Lindsey Unified School District, 79–80

Lytle, James "Torch," 18

Maddin, Brent, 51
managed instruction, 11
Manno, Bruno, 51–52
Martinez, Brenda, 20, 39
Martinez, Charles, 51
Maryland, 74
Matheison, Julie, 22–23
McDonald, Tim, 47, 48
memoranda of understandings (MOUs), 3, 19
Miami-Dade County Public Schools, 80
Milwaukee school district, 2–3, 19–20, 43
mindset barrier, 11–14, 23, 47, 64
Minnesota Legislature, 48
Minnesota New Country School (MNCS), 1–2, 14, 26–27, 27
Moe, Terry, 61–62
Morial, Marc, 73
Morris, Edmund, 71
motivation, student, xxii, xxv, 8, 69

Nathan, Joe, 49
National Alliance for Public Charter Schools, xxiv, 57–58
National Association of Charter School Authorizers, 58
National Charter Schools Alliance, 57
National Commission on Excellence in Education, 71
National Council on Teacher Quality`, 49
National Education Association (NEA), 19, 61
A Nation at Risk (National Commission on Excellence in Education), 71
Nazareno, Lori, 28
New Schools Venture Fund, 58
New Teacher Project (NTP), 52
New York City PROSE schools, 21–22, 81

No Child Left Behind (NCLB, 2001), 10, 63, 71
Nordgren, Lynn, 67

O'Day, Jennifer, 71
O'Donnell, Patrick, 81
Olsen, Anders, xxii
Olson, Ruth Ann, 26
one-room schools, xxiii, xxiv
online education: benefits of, 54–55, 79; investment in, 79–80; during pandemic, 56, 77–78, 79; predictions for, 54
Osborne, David, 15, 16, 81–82
Ouchi, William, 26

Pai, Ananth, 16–18
pandemic: achievement gap exposed by, 78; by-pass possibility and, xxvi, 56; equity issues exposed by, 80; nature of schooling changed by, 64, 66, 81; school adaptations during, 56, 77–78, 79–80, 81; societal impact of, 77–79; student motivation during, xxii; students with special needs and, 78, 79; teacher retention and, 35
parents, xxv, 4, 29, 31, 43, 67
Park, Jeff, 38
Parr, Cris, xxi–xxii, 1–3, 19
Parr, John, 19
Patashnik, Eric, 47
Perpich, Rudy, xxi
Phi Delta Kappan (PDK), 28, 29
pilot schools, 16, 20, 57
Pondiscio, Robert, 80
Premack, Eric, 67
principals, 6–7, 11
Pritchett, Henry, 70
Program for International Student Assessment (PISA), xxii
PROSE schools, 21–22, 81
Public Agenda Foundation, 28, 29
public education: autonomy and authority in, 9, 10, 16–17, 66; change in, 38, 54–56, 64–67, 80–81;

equity issues in, 32, 37, 73, 80; "real school" expectations for, 23, 47, 64, 70; rules governing structure of, 69–70; standardization of, 11, 71; teacher accountability lacking in, 9–10; teacher retention and satisfaction in, 7, 29, *33*, 35, *36*
publicity, 41, 42–43, 62

race, 71–73
"real school" mindset: as barrier to teacher-powered schools, 23, 47, 64, 70; disrupted by pandemic, 78, 80
Reinventing America's Schools (Osborne), 15, 16
Relay Graduate Education School, 48–49, 51
religious schooling, 65
retirement programs, 47–48
Ricker, Mary Cathryn, 7
Rosenstock, Larry, 50, 59

Samuels, Christina, 72
Sanders, Ted, 9
San Francisco Community School, 26
Schleicher, Andreas, 80–81
school, changing nature of, 64–66, 81
school districts, 55–57, 65
School for Urban Planning and Architecture (SUPAR), 3
Schroeder, Jon, 57
S-curves, 54, 55
Sedatis, Chris, 8
self-improvement, 12–13, 15, 48
Seubert, Liz, 23
"Seventeen Reasons Why Football Is Better Than High School" (Childress), 13
Shanker, Albert, 59, 67, 68
Shindler, John, 32–33
Skria, Linda, 32
Smith, Marshall, 71
Smith, Nelson, 57
Snyder, Taryn, 21, 59
social media, 42–43

Solloum, Serena, 32
South Dakota schools, 22–23
special needs, students with, 22, 27, 78, 79
sports, 13, 70
Springfield, Massachusetts, 82
standardized testing, 10, 44
Steiner, Cordell, 17–18
Steps Guide to Creating a Teacher-Powered School (Farris-Berg, Nazareno), 28
Strembitsky, Michael, 18–19
student motivation, xxii, xxv, 8, 69
student performance: achievement gap in, 71–72; autonomy and, 14, 31–34, 72; in charter schools, 58; evaluating, 44–45, 58; teacher quality and, 37
Summit Schools, 71
Sundin, Louise, 67, 75

Target, 74–75
teacher leadership, 4, *5*, 10–11
Teacher Powered Initiative, 28
teacher-powered schools: accountability in, 7, 68; achievement gap addressed by, 72; autonomy and authority in, xxi, 14–15, 16, 26, 68; collaboration in, 7; EE network for, xiv; extra work required in, 7, 11, 19, 20, 34, 47, 64; fundamentals of, xxi–xxii; parent support for, xxv, 4, 29, 31, 43, 67; principals' roles in, 6–7; public interest in, *6*, *31*; self-improvement in, 12–13, 15; student-centered nature of, xxiii, 7–8, 15, 21; student motivation in, 8, 69; teacher certification in, 75; teacher interest in, xxiv–xxv, 4, *6*, 28–30, *31*; teacher retention in, 64, 73; teacher satisfaction in, 7–8, 19, 33, *33*, 34; union debates over, 62, 64; union opposition to, xxvii, 3, 19–20, 61, 67; union support for, 21, 67, 68, 82; variability among, 59

teacher-powered schools movement: administrative resistance to, 9, 10; *vs.* change-everything assumption, 74; characteristics of, 25–26, 27–28; *vs.* charter school movement, 58; distortions in, 57–60; documenting, 41, 44; funding and, xxvi, 41, 47, 65, 72; growth of, 4, 28–29, 53, 58–59, 60; institutional resistance to, 18, 37, 38; measuring student performance for, 41, 44–45; mindset barrier to, 11–14, 23, 47, 64; naming of, 4; organizational space for, 74; origins of, xxv–xxvi, 26–28; potential by-passing and, xxvi, 53–57, 66; publicity for, 41–43, 62; regional networks for, 41, 45–46; replicating success within, 59–60; retirement programs and, 41, 47–48; teacher burnout and, 47; teacher leadership in, *5*, 10–11; teacher preparation and, 41, 48–51; teacher unions and, xxvii, 19–20, 43; teacher views on, 4–8
"teacher-powered" term usage, 28
teacher practices, 28
teacher retention, 34–36, *36*, 42, 64, 73
teachers: changing roles of, 64; education of, 41, 48–51; job satisfaction/dissatisfaction of, 7–8, 19, 29, 33, *33*, 35; minority, 72–73; perceived as average, 12, 66; professional standards for, 37, 49, 62, 65, 75; unaware of teacher-powered option, xxv, 41; views on teacher-powered schools, xxiv–xxv, 4, *6*, 28–30, *31*
Teachers as Owners (ed. Dirkswager), xxvi, 28
Teacher Union Reform Network (TURN), xxvii
teacher unions: change within, 3, 43, 62; changing context for, 65–66; criticism of, 61; declining membership of, 66; legal/structural barriers to, 42; No Child Left Behind opposed by, 10, 63; pilot schools supported by, 20–21; in publicity efforts, 42, 43, 62; teacher-powered schools debated by, 62, 64; teacher-powered schools opposed by, xxvii, 3, 19–20, 61, 67; teacher-powered schools supported by, 21, 67, 68, 82; transformative potential of, 61, 62, 63–65, 67–68; trench warfare of, xxvii, 63
Teach for America, 52
teaching models, 4–5, 11
technology, 36, 65–66
Thinking Out the How (Kolderie), 58
Thomas, Dee, 14–15
Thomas, Doug, 50
Tinkering Toward Utopia (Tyack, Cuban), 69
Toch, Tom, 37, 60
Transformative Classroom Management (Shindler), 32–33
Trusting Teachers with School Success (Farris-Berg, Dirkswager), xxvi, 25, 28
Tweed, Paul, 23
Tyack, David, 69

unions. *See* teacher unions
United Federation of Teachers (UFT), 21
University of Texas College of Education, 51
Urban Assembly School for Green Careers (UAGC), 8, 22
U.S. Supreme Court, 65

Victory School, 1
Vitrella, Alex, 29

Wagner, Tony, 49
Walsh, Kate, 49
Walton, Sam, 74
Washor, Eliot, 59
Weingarten, Randi, 66, 67
West Virginia, 42

Whalen, Nora, 11
Who Controls Teachers' Work? (Ingersoll), xiv
"Why Don't Struggling K-12 Districts Just Dissolve?" (Burnett), 56
Widmeyer, Scott (Widmeyer Communications): on Avalon School management meetings, 39; on awareness of teacher-powered option, xxv, 41; on support for teacher-powered schools, 4, 28–29, 30–31
Wildlands School, 23
Williams, Joe, 52
Wise, Art, 66–67
workforce, preparing students for, xxiv
Wright, John, 42, 61
Wright Brothers, 12

www.ingramcontent.com/pod-product-compliance
Lightning Source LLC
Chambersburg PA
CBHW020750230426
43665CB00009B/564